Main sites of prehistoric art

ck engravings

Grotte Kapova

Domestic art
of Central Europe

Neolithic statuettes

monica valley
lley

Malta

Cyclades statuettes

Neolithic figurines
and statues

rvings

Cave art of
Southern Africa

Kenniff cave

Aboriginal cave art

Koonalda cave

Original edition published 1986 by Casterman, Tournai
© 1986 Casterman

This edition published 1990 by Franklin Watts
© 1990 Franklin Watts

Franklin Watts
96 Leonard Street
London EC2A 4RH

ISBN: 0 86313 987 6

Editor: Jenny Wood

Picture credits
Photothèque France-U.R.S.S.: page 9. C.N.D.P./J. Vertut: pages 18, 24.
C.N.D.P./M. Pialoux: pages 20, 34, 64l. C.N.D.P./Tendron: page 32.D.
Lavallée: page 38. Musée de Préhistoire de Nemours: pages 41, 64r,
74t. Giraudon: page 44. M. Boureux (Fouilles URA n° 12 du C.N.R.S.):
page 48. C.D.P.A.-D.R.: pages 54, 56. Michel Pierre: pages 61, 62 (3
ph.), 72t, 73. Roger-Viollet: pages 66, 68 (2 ph.), 69. Ferrero/Labat/
Explorer: page 70t. Casterman: pages 70b, 71. Ph. Andrieux: page 72b.
Laboratoire de Géologie du Quaternaire – M. Taïeb: pages 74 (2ph.),
75. D. Serrette/M.N.H.N.: page 76.

Printed in Portugal

THE FIRST SETTLEMENTS

FRANKLIN WATTS
London • New York • Toronto • Sydney

CONTENTS

PREFACE

This book covers about 35,000 years – no more than one per cent of the whole of human history. Even so, it was time enough for the lives of over 1,000 generations.

All the changes described in this book happened in prehistoric times. Pre-history is the name given to the periods before people left any written records of their lives. There are, however, many other forms of evidence about our prehistoric ancestors. Many of the places where they made homes, hunted and worshipped have been found. Archaeologists work carefully on these sites to uncover remains of tools, houses, weapons and clothes. At the end of this book there is a section called 'Researching the past' which describes the methods they use.

The first people you meet in this book are men and women from the later years of the Old Stone Age. This period of pre-history gets its name from the kind of stone tools that have been found, and is often known as the Palaeolithic Age from two Greek words meaning stone and old. The Old Stone Age stretched back hundreds of thousands of years but it was only in the last part, or Upper Palaeolithic times, that our direct ancestors appeared. They are often described as hunter-gatherers, and the first part of the book describes their lives around 30,000 years ago. In Part 2 we see how settlements began, with people staying in one place for only a season then settling all year round.

Part 3 shows how people in different parts of the world had different ways of growing crops and keeping animals, and describes the development of villages and settlements. People began to acquire new skills such as pottery, weaving and the use of bronze and iron, along with new forms of knowledge such as astronomy. Some of these changes are described in Part 4, which brings the human story up to the last few centuries BC.

THE LAST ICE AGE

The first Ice Age began over 1 million years ago. Since then there have been seven Ice Ages. During each of these, the earth's climate became much colder, and huge areas of sea and land were covered with a blanket of ice. In some places the ice was hundreds of metres deep.

The last Ice Age lasted for about 65,000 years and ended only 10,000 years ago. Two enormous sheets of ice covered North America as far south as New York and all of Northern Europe. They were joined by a permanent layer of ice called an ice cap, which covered the whole of the North Atlantic. Further south, in the Pyrenees mountains between France and Spain, there were glaciers (rivers of ice) almost fifty kilometres long. Even the island of Corsica in the Mediterranean was affected.

The oceans were very cold. Icebergs drifted as far south as Spain. The sea level dropped, to almost 100 metres lower than it is today. The North Sea disappeared altogether, apart from a lake at the north which joined with the ice around the North Pole.

The map below shows the ice cap as it was at the peak of the last Ice Age, 20,000 years ago. The other map shows the ice cap today.

When the earth grew colder and the ice cap spread, animal life was obviously affected. In America, because the mountain ranges run from north to south, animals were able to escape down the valleys to warmer lands. But in Europe and Asia, where the mountains run from east to west, animals found it more difficult to escape and many died.

The natural habitat of reindeer today are the forests and clearings of Lapland in northern Scandinavia. Reindeer survive in snow-covered land by eating moss and leaves. During the last Ice Ace, the best place to find this vegetation was in south-west France.

HUNTER-GATHERERS 30,000 YEARS AGO

The first human-type creatures appeared in different places on earth more than 2½ million years ago. We give them the scientific name, *Homo erectus*, meaning 'upright being'. They were replaced by *Homo sapiens*, or 'knowing being', who first appeared at the beginning of the last Ice Age.

Homo erectus used stones picked up from the ground as simple tools. Later, people began to choose stones of different shapes for different jobs and later still they learned how to chip these stones into the shape of an axe or a knife.

Towards the end of the Old Stone Age, people were able to shape fine blades out of a type of stone called flint, which splits easily, and also out of bone. They made scrapers with curved edges, throwing sticks and tips for spears as well as tools for engraving patterns on to bone or for piercing holes in skins to make clothes.

In Europe, people with these skills lived south of the ice all the way from Spain to the lands around the Danube river. They were hunter-gatherers, living in widely scattered groups. Each family might roam each year over great distances, sheltering where they could, gathering seeds or fruit and killing animals.

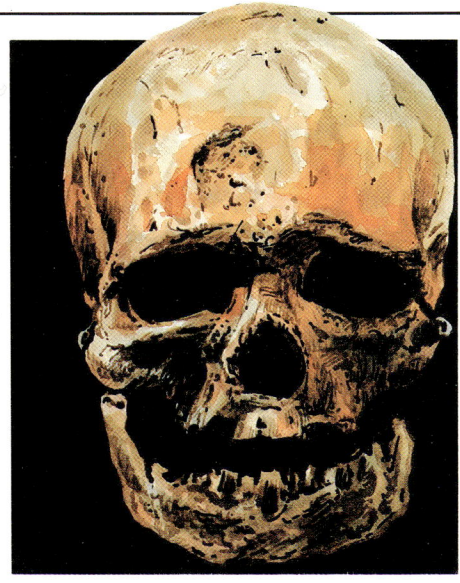

This skull was found in 1868 at a place called Cro-Magnon in the Dordogne region of France. Scientists believe it is the skull of a true *Homo sapiens*. It is the same size as skulls found at Neanderthal in Germany in 1858, but it has a higher forehead and a shorter chin. Scientists think that Cro-Magnon people were probably between 1.7 and 1.9m tall, and that they resembled modern human beings more closely than did the so-called 'Neanderthal Man'.

Although south-western France lay south of the edge of the great ice cap, the weather was cold. The plateaux were bare, and trees grew only in the valleys.

The hunting band sometimes went out to kill large animals such as horses, bison, reindeer or even mammoths. Sometimes they managed to trap only a young wolf or a rabbit. The hunters wore sturdy leather garments and necklaces of stag or wolf teeth. Leather pouches held all they needed.

Their spears had flint blades strapped tightly to the shafts. The men spent more time crouching round the fire making weapons and tools than walking in search of food. Several skeletons from this period show that spines were damaged from sitting for too long.

HUNTING THE MAMMOTH

The hunter-gatherers of the late Old Stone Age used a variety of weapons. The simplest was the short wooden spear fitted with a pointed flint blade. It was used to kill animals at close range and to finish off wounded prey. There were also lighter throwing spears with points of ivory or reindeer horn. The hunter-gatherers invented the spear-thrower, a type of sling which helped them hurl the spear much further and faster.

It is likely that the hunters also made spears and clubs of wood which they hardened in the fire, yet no traces have been found of such weapons. Flint, bone and ivory survive for thousands of years, but leather and wood rot away. So we cannot tell how these hunters trapped animals. They probably used leather nooses which caught the animal by the neck or foot, but all traces of these have disappeared.

Hunters in some regions ambushed larger animals such as reindeer, bison and horses on well-used tracks such as water-crossings. Sometimes they drove their prey into a narrow ravine from which there was no escape. But we can never know exactly how they killed enormous beasts such as the rhinoceros and the mammoth. These were far more dangerous than reindeer or horses, and spears would not have gone through their tough hides. The remains at some sites suggest that hunters may have driven the animals into swamps where their great weight bogged them down and made them easier to kill.

It is also difficult to know how often hunters came across these huge beasts. Nor do we know whether they found them by accident or whether the animals were tracked on purpose and killed for their bones which some groups used for building materials.

The mammoth was the largest of the prehistoric animals. It lived in Europe and in Siberia, the eastern part of the Soviet Union.

Mammoths were a kind of elephant which evolved over millions of years from small beasts with long muzzles. About 10 million years ago they grew warm, hairy coats and developed smaller ears.

Mammoths are well-known today from frozen specimens that lay for more than 30,000 years in parts of Siberia which are never free from frost. The deep cold preserved them so well that it has even been possible to see the tree shoots and pine needles in their stomachs.

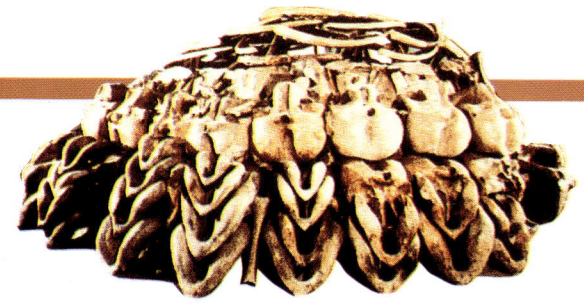

A BONE AND IVORY HUT

This hut, made entirely of mammoth bones, was found at Mezhirich in the part of the Soviet Union called the Ukraine. Tusks were used for the framework and these were then covered with ninety-five jaw bones. The hut was more than 11m² in area and there were several shallow hearths dug in the earth. There is a reconstruction of the hut in the museum in Kiev.

HUNTING THE REINDEER

Between 16,000 and 9,000 BC the people of the Old Stone Age seem to have relied on one animal for food, clothing and bone to make scrapers, needles and fish-hooks. The bones found in many prehistoric sites, especially those in south-west France, show that this animal was the reindeer. At Lascaux, ninety-eight per cent of the bones of grass-eating animals came from reindeer while at La Madeleine the figure is between eighty-nine and ninety-seven per cent. The finds at La Madeleine give the time from 16,000 to 9,000 BC its name of the Magdalenian period.

Although reindeer remains are the most common finds at prehistoric sites, some groups of people specialised in other species. Nearly ninety per cent of bones found in the Gironde region of France were from bison. At one site in the Dordogne nearly all the bones came from rabbits.

Sites from the last centuries of the Magdalenian period are usually larger than earlier ones and are also closer together. It seems that the population was growing and that people were beginning to settle in one place or changing their home only a few times each year. In central France, some Magdalenian people set up hunting camps in the spring and autumn to slay reindeer as they migrated south and north with the changing weather. In south-west France, the reindeer could live all year and here people began to make permanent homes. They may even have begun to keep the animals in herds.

Some settled people became skilled fishers. From about 15,000 BC they used harpoons with a double row of barbs at the tip and a hole at the end of the shaft. A leather thong was passed through the hole and used for hauling fish out of the water.

This picture reconstructs the scene at Pincevent in central France, where there was a crossing over the river Seine. Magdalenian people put up their tents in May and November to surprise the reindeer as they crossed the river in the spring and returned in the autumn.

THE WOUNDED REINDEER

This outline of a fallen reindeer was cut into the walls of a cave at Ariège in France. The drawing is about 60cm long and is in a panel along with fourteen others. Many other prehistoric cave drawings have been found, yet few show reindeers despite the fact that they seem to have been the main hunted animal.

The reindeer hunted by prehistoric people were almost exactly the same as those found in northern Europe today. Their size varied according to the climate. In periods when it was not only cold but also very dry or very damp, the remains show that they were smaller and fewer in number. During the Magdalenian period, at the very end of the Ice Age, the climate in south-west France was ideal and the reindeer grew in size and numbers.

THE FIRST HOUSES

An important development for some prehistoric people came when they began to improve the hollows in the ground and the caves which provided natural shelters. In many parts of Europe, caves have been found with the remains of skins stretched over a framework of mammoth tusks. One cave, at Arcy sur Curé in eastern France, has small stone slabs laid down to make a kind of tiled floor. Another early form of dwelling was sunk into the cave floor. A cave near Santandar in Spain has a rectangular hole almost thirty centimetres deep, five metres long and two metres wide. Even in this small space there was a hearth along one side and, opposite, a heap of earth that was probably used as a seat or bed. Flint chippings have been found among the charred wood in the hearth. Someone must have sat there to chip and shape flint tools by the heat and light of the fire.

Where there were no caves, people often set their homes deep into the ground to protect themselves from the weather. The sunken part might go a metre into the ground and have steps leading down to the floor where the hearth was. In eastern Europe and in the Soviet Union, a circle of mammoth bones was placed around the base of a hut to keep out the cold. At one site in Czechoslovakia, thirteen of these sunken homes edged with mammoth bones have been found.

By about 25,000 years ago, some prehistoric buildings had become larger and more complicated than the first simple huts. A huge prehistoric site on the banks of the river Don in the southern Soviet Union has the remains of one of these large buildings. It was oval in shape, forty metres long and eighteen metres wide. There were several round hollows in the ground which may have been used for storing food. Down the centre was a row of nine hearths. Some prehistorians have suggested that the building must have been a communal home shared by several families, although this is impossible to prove.

Stone was used for building about 23,000 years ago at Vigne-Brun on sloping ground above the river Loire in France. The people who settled here began by digging into the slope to make a level floor about four metres across. They then used blocks of stone to make solid walls. The huts were probably finished off with a roof of animal hides stretched over a wooden framework. Five or six of these dwellings seem to have been occupied at the same time. Like the large house on the river Don, the stone huts at Vigne-Brun may have been a settlement for a group of people who lived together permanently or for several months at a time.

The first building materials often came from animals which were hunted or died naturally. Mammoth tusks made a framework which could be covered with reindeer skins. Jaw and leg bones were used to strengthen the base.

This rock face near the river Allier in France was a site of stone-built homes for several thousand years. One of the dwellings was almost 8m long, nearly 5m wide and had five hearths.

Twenty-three thousand years ago, people settled at Vigne-Brun above the river Loire in France, even though the ground was covered with snow and ice for much of the year. They protected themselves against the cold by building stone walls below skin roofs. They gathered wood for their fires, and collected six different kinds of flints from as far as 300km away.

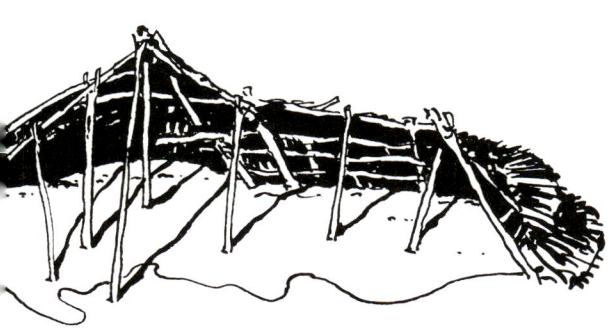

A reconstruction of a partly sunken building in Czechoslovakia, between 20,000 and 25,000 years ago. Several dwellings were built close to each other and the whole settlement was surrounded by a fence or ditch.

BEAUTIFYING THE LIVING AND THE DEAD

Pictures of prehistoric people used to show them half-naked or covered with just a few, badly-fastened animal skins, and with dirty, straggling hair. But they could not have protected themselves against the cold of the Ice Age unless their clothes were carefully sewn together and fastened, and remains in prehistoric sites show it is much more likely that clothes were well-fitting and that people cared for their hair and their general appearance.

The best examples come from graves which have been found at Sungir in the Soviet Union. In one, there was the skeleton of a man whose body had been sprinkled with ochre (an earth containing iron which is used to make yellow or red dyes). On the body there were rows of bone beads and buttons. Their position shows that they were sewn on to garments which have since rotted away. The man must have worn some kind of jacket or parka, trousers and boots.

At the other end of Europe, at Grimaldi in north-west Italy, a skeleton was found with its skull covered by dozens of tiny shells. These must have been held in place by some sort of hairnet. Another skull at Liguria, also in Italy, had hundreds of small shells, deer teeth and tiny bone pendants engraved with pictures. Other, similar, skeletons have been found, some with larger pendants which hung down the sides and over the forehead. These pendants were made from bone and ivory, large shells and the long, pointed teeth of deer and foxes. Head-dresses like this are found mostly on male skeletons. Women seem to have worn only the smaller hair decorations, held in place by a net, headband or cap.

One grave in Liguria clearly shows the differences between the head-dresses of males and females. The corpses of a man, woman and teenage boy were found lying side by side. All wore head-dresses of small seashells and fish bones but the man's also had ivory drops and deer teeth hanging over his forehead. He and the teenage boy wore necklaces and deer teeth at their throats. The woman had no necklaces and just a single ivory pendant at her throat.

Prehistoric people wore bracelets, too. One of the men buried at Sungir had fine bracelets carved from mammoth tusks on each elbow and wrist. In Liguria men, women and children wore shell bracelets at their elbows and wrists. Only men were allowed to wear decorations around their feet, ankles and knees.

Examples of late Old Stone Age ornaments: shells, animal teeth, the hollow bones of birds and pieces of bone decorated with pictures of animals. The well-worn holes show that these ornaments were everyday wear.

This lady is known as the 'Venus of Brassempouy'. Her name comes from the place in south-west France where she was found. She was carved in ivory about 25,000 years ago and is only 3.8m high. The carvings on her head show that her hair was carefully dressed or that she wore a hood.

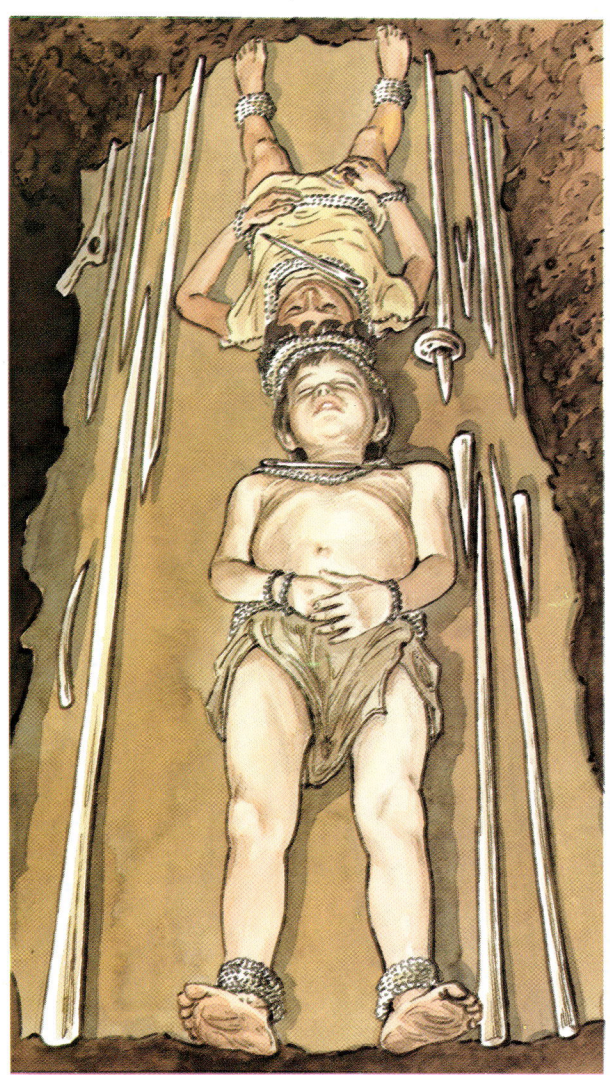

A reconstruction of a grave at Sungir, where two children were found buried head to head. Around the heads were ivory beads, foxes' teeth and half hoops of ivory. The children wore bracelets around their wrists and rings on their fingers. Piles of beads were found at their feet and bone needles had been placed under their chins.

SKETCHES OF BODIES IN OLD STONE AGE GRAVES
Top left: man
Top right: two children
Centre top: woman and child
Centre left to right: three women
Bottom left: child
Bottom right: man

19

THE ART OF STONE-CUTTING

When archaeologists open a prehistoric site they almost always uncover stone remains. As well as tools, spearheads and scrapers there is usually a lot of waste made up of the pieces which were chipped and flaked away from lumps of hard stone. These finds do not mean that prehistoric people used only stone. They probably used just as much wood. Some of them made cloth out of fibres collected from plants and from the skins of animals. But the wood and the fibres have decayed over the years.

Because stone is the main material left, we have to learn as much as we can from it. Prehistorians try to group the various kinds of stone remains according to their shape, what they were used for, how they were made and their age. This helps to build up a picture of how people lived at different times.

By careful study of the tools and piles of waste, experts can show how prehistoric stone-cutters worked. Their most important skill was knapping flint. Flint is a kind of quartz, a hard rock which often appears in lumps of softer stone. Knapping began by chipping the flint 'core' out of the softer stone. Then the knapper had to knock slices, or blades, of flint off the core. These blades were then turned into spearheads, scrapers and other useful tools.

The first man-made tools were very crude. This scraper was made well over 50,000 years ago. All the stone-cutter did was to chip the edge of the flint until it was sharp.

Starting work. The tool-maker removes a flint and starts shaping it. At his feet are some hammers, some blades he has already made and piles of waste stone.

KNAPPING FLINTS

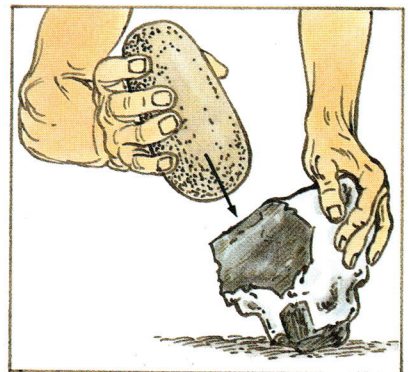

Knocking out the core

Shaping the edge of the core

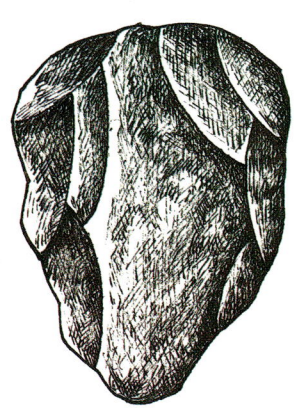

The core removed

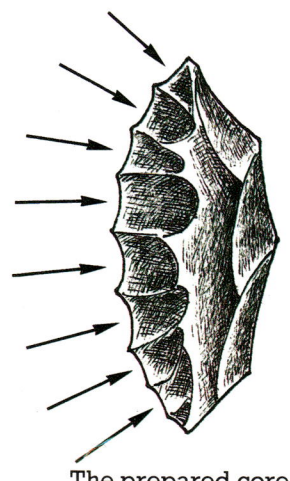

The prepared core

Between about 20,000 and 16,000 BC, people of the Solutrean culture in southern France and northern Spain specialised in making finely patterned blades by 'pressure-flaking'. The workman is carefully pressing small flakes off the edge of the flint with a piece of reindeer horn. At his feet are an uncut blade, some willow leaf blades which were a Solutrean speciality, two spearheads and two sticks.

Below: both sides of a spearhead

Knocking off the first blade

Preparing to strike another blade

Core (front and side)

Chipping off an unwanted piece to make knapping easier

The knapping continues

The used core. Each core usually gave between ten and twenty blades

A blade struck from the core

Blades (fronts and side)

21

THE FIRST ARTISTS

The first known attempts at art have been found in caves in the limestone hills of the Périgord region of France, the northern mountains of Spain and a few sites in Italy. Thirty thousand years ago, Palaeolithic people used hand-axes to engrave figures in the soft limestone. Sometimes there are traces of paint within the carved outlines. The figures are crudely drawn but it is possible to see that they are mostly intended to be females or animals.

These earliest-known paintings were made near the mouths of caves. About 17,000 years ago, artists of the Magdalenian culture began to work in places which are often so far inside the earth that they can be reached only by experienced potholers. The most famous paintings have been found in the network of caves at Lascaux in the Périgord. They date from between 17,000 and 11,000 years ago. Apart from Lascaux, over 150 caves with paintings from the same period have been found in France, Spain and Italy.

The artists of the Magdalenian period worked in passages where no one can stand upright,or on cave roofs which they reached by tree ladders. Why did they put their pictures where very few would ever see them? It may be that these early people thought of caves as the womb of the earth, the place where the first living creatures came from. The artists may have believed that they could make life return to the earth each spring by filling the cave womb with lifelike pictures of the animals they depended on for food and clothing.

The painters used animal-hair brushes, horse-hair pads and hollow bones for blow-spraying coloured powders. They made yellows, reds and browns from ochre. Black came from charcoal, and white from chalk or china clay.

Using a tree ladder to paint on a cave roof. Painters sometimes used scaffolding or ropes. At Lascaux the imprint of a rope was found, as well as some holes bored high up in a wall.

THE WONDERS OF LASCAUX

Two of the famous Lascaux paintings show a cow and a horse. Signs are painted on and around the animals. You can see a thin line on the cow's rump and a roundish mark on the horse's shoulder. Artists in other regions used different symbols on their paintings.

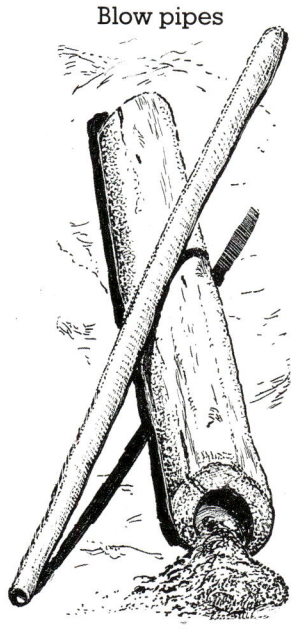

Blow pipes

In some caves you can find outlines of hands which show up like the negatives of a photograph. The artist pressed the model's hand against the wall and sprayed over it through a blow pipe. The hands are usually small and look like the hands of women or children. In some, the fingers seem to have been cut short. It is possible that the women or children gave their fingers as sacrifices to the spirit of the cave to make sure that spring and the birth of new animals followed the long, cold winter.

The painter uses a brush made from a plant stem while his assistant holds a blazing torch which has been dipped in animal fat. Some of these torches have been found in caves. Nearly all the cave paintings show animals such as bisons and horses.

ART AROUND THE WORLD

Artists in the Périgord were scratching the first picture outlines about 30,000 years ago. At about the same time, other people in southern Germany, in the fertile areas near the Danube, were learning to use bone and ivory tusks to make small statuettes. The oldest of these figures which we can recognise today are miniature carvings of horses, bison, mammoths and people.

But Europe was not the only part of the world where art was developing. Fragments of painted rock of nearly the same age have been found in north-eastern Brazil. By the time of the Magdalenian cave painters, Brazilian artists were also decorating caves. Two hundred of them have been found, dating back 12,000 years, with figures of men, animals and trees.

Stone Age people in Africa were painters, too. An important part of what we know about their life comes from rock paintings. Some of the most exciting pictures in Africa are found in the Tassili hills deep in the Sahara desert. Six thousand years ago this was a land of flowing rivers and green pastures. Tassili people painted their caves with lively pictures of men, animals and gods. The human figures show that black people then lived in the Sahara, where today the few inhabitants are Arabs.

Some forms of Stone Age art remain alive today among groups who follow a hunter-gathering way of life. For example, some Bushmen in southern Africa are rock painters, as are some Aborigines in Australia. Aboriginal art goes back a very long way. Some engravings on rocks in north-eastern Australia are at least 20,000 years old.

BRAZIL: MONSTERS AND PEOPLE
Cave paintings in Brazil often show processions of people or very small people overshadowed by monster-sized animals. This kind of art died out a few centuries before the birth of Christ.

FRANCE: THE DAPPLED HORSES OF PECH-MERLE

These horses were painted about 18,000 BC. The painter used the shape of the rock face to outline the horses on the left. There are also several 'negative' hand prints on the rock, but none have fingers missing.

FRANCE: FINGER SCRATCHES AT GARGAS
Cave art does not always consist of finished paintings. Fingermarks are often found on clay-type surfaces. They may have been made for amusement, as a way of decorating a dark passageway or as a religious symbol. Some appear with rough sketches for a nearby wall painting and may have been a kind of practice work. At Gargas in the Pyrenees in southern France, there is a whole cave wall of finger scratches.

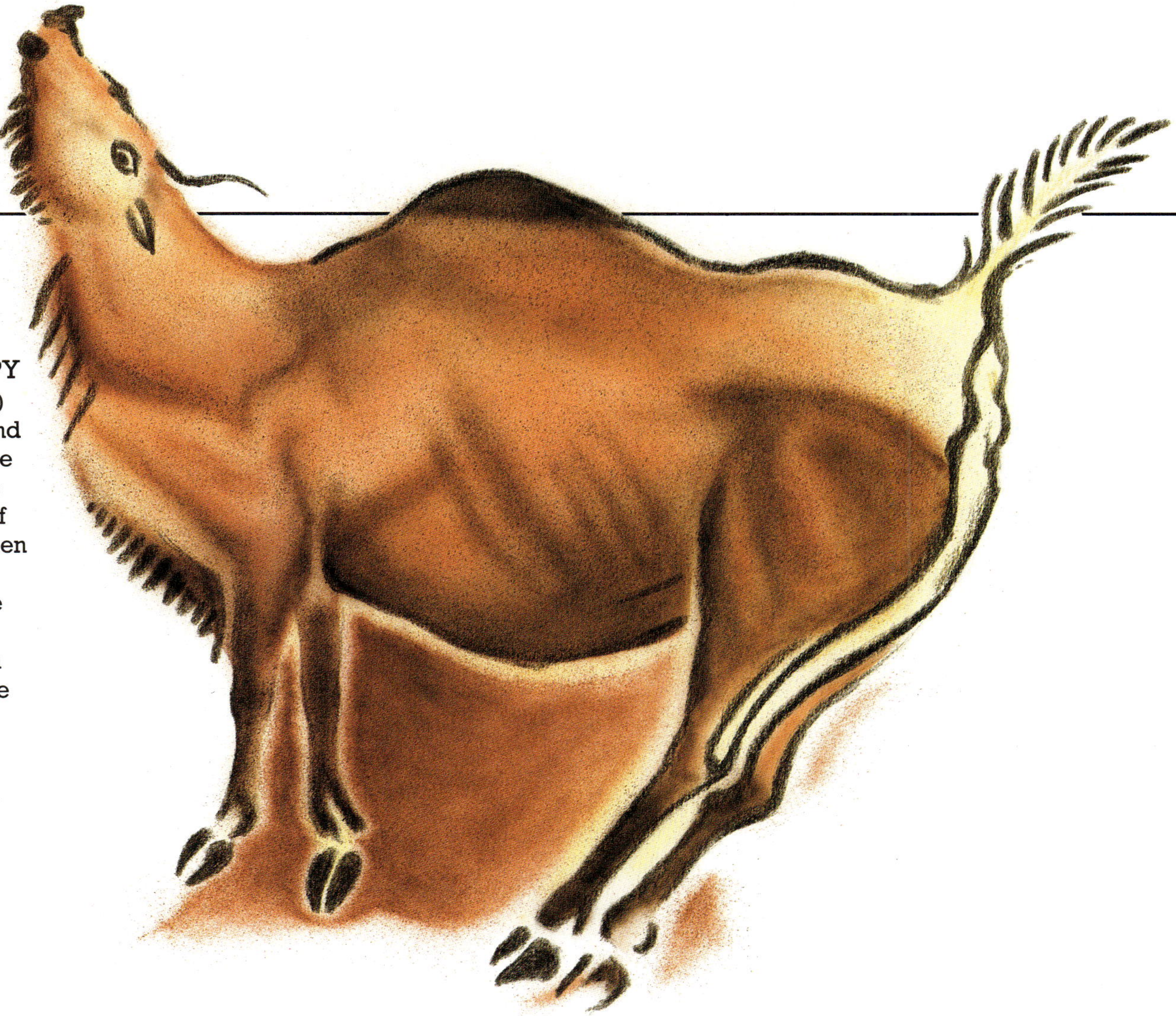

SPAIN:
THE ABBÉ BREUIL'S COPY

The Abbé Breuil (1877-1961) was a pioneer in studying and dating the work of Stone Age artists. He spent much of his life making careful copies of the paintings. Copying is often a better way than photography of showing the tiniest details, especially if figures have been drawn on top of each other. This is one of the Abbé's paintings showing a bison on a cave roof at Altamira in northern Spain.

AFRICA: PAINTING FROM THE TASSILI

There are several styles of Tassili art. This is one in the 'round-headed men' style. It was the work of black people who then lived in the area. It suggests that they had the custom of painting their bodies. The large figure may be a god.

BEGINNINGS OF SETTLEMENT
THE FORD AT PINCEVENT

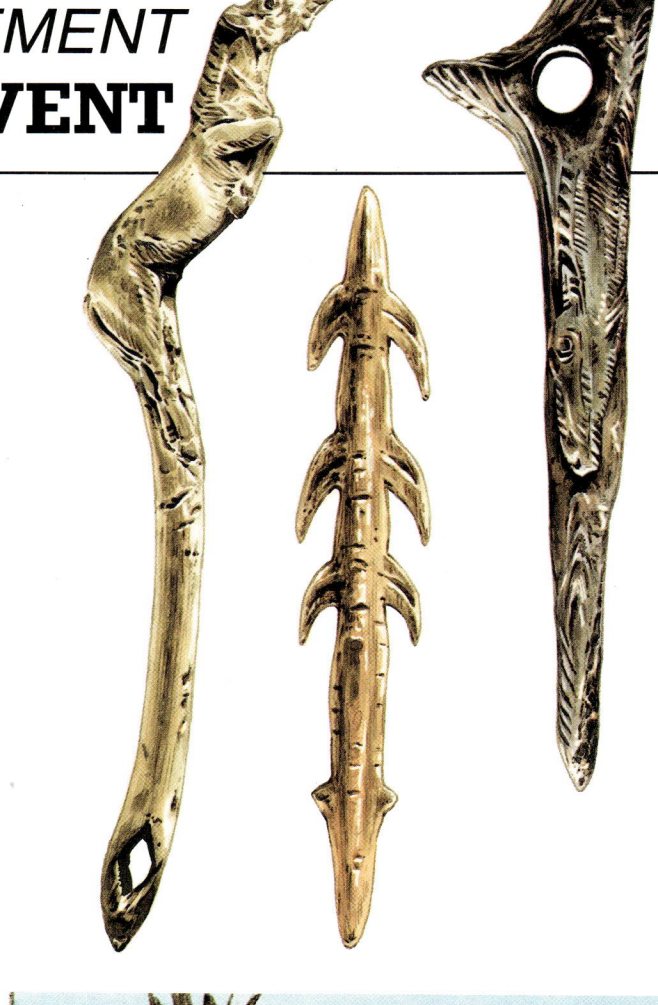

In 1964, gravel-digging machines were working at Pincevent on the banks of the river Seine about sixty kilometres southeast of Paris. Just in time, a team of archaeologists uncovered the remains of a camp used by Magdalenian people about 13,000 years ago. There were at least thirteen dwellings, and it was clear that up to five of them were lived in at the same time. The site showed so much about the lives of the Magdalenians that the gravel-diggers left thousands of square metres for the archaeologists to continue their work.

It was soon clear that there had been a ford at Pincevent from prehistoric times until the river flow changed a few centuries ago. Reindeer used the ford to cross the Seine when they moved south in November and returned to the north in May. Magdalenian families came here for a few days or weeks to kill reindeer. It seems that about a month was the time needed to kill between fifteen and twenty reindeer. No one knows where they came from or where they went when the reindeer migration was over.

The prehistoric visitors put up oval-shaped tents and built hearths just outside the entrances. Much of our knowledge of their lives in and around these homes comes from careful studies of their litter. The excavators made plans of the position of rubbish such as bones, ash, and scraps from flint workings. The stone-cutters seem to have done their work over animal skins so they could carry all the waste a short distance from the tent. Other waste, such as bones and ashes, was thrown away from the fire. This information makes it possible to work out the position and shape of the tents from where the rubbish fell. The shattered remains of the stones which were used to heat food and drink also provide clues. These often splintered in the fire so they were thrown away and replaced with fresh stones.

During their short stay in the camp, the Magdalenian people seem to have spent all their time on work connected with reindeer hunting. By looking at the flint remains under a microscope, we can see that the stone-cutters made the tools they needed on the spot. There are tiny traces of fresh skin, meat and bones which show that some flints were used to cut meat, while others were scrapers to clean the skins. Some flints are in the shape of very fine blades. These have grooves to fit into the shafts of throwing spears, which would have been the hunters' main weapon.

Bone implements made by Magdalenians in other parts of France about 10,000 years ago. *(Right)* a pierced tool which may have been used to straighten spear shafts as they were heated. *(Centre)* a harpoon for catching fish. *(Left)* a spear-thrower. *Below:* how spear-throwers were used.

Women may have done work such as scraping hides, preparing fish and stitching clothes.

The archaeologists at Pincevent believed that the Magdalenians made tents from a framework of poles covered with reindeer hides stitched together. The hearths were placed near the fronts of the tents and were cleaned out every so often.

A HOUSE ON THE BANKS OF THE RHINE

In 1968, builders were digging a foundation for a new house on a hillside overlooking the Rhine river at Gönnersdorf, about fifteen kilometres outside Koblenz in Germany. They came across the ruins of homes which had been lived in about 10,400 BC. The site lies along a shelf about forty metres above the river. Nothing like it has been found anywhere else in Europe, apart from its twin site, Andernach, which lies on the opposite bank of the river.

Archaeologists moved in and carefully uncovered the floors of three large, circular huts, each between six and eight metres in diameter. They also found stone wedges where posts had been placed into the ground to support the roof and walls. The posts were covered with animal skins which almost certainly came from a type of miniature horse called Przewalski. Large quantities of Przewalski bones have been found around the site. About forty hides would have been needed to cover the framework of each hut, twenty-three of them for the roof.

In each hut, most of the floor was paved with hundreds of pieces of slate. Altogether, about 500 of these were engraved with simple, badly-drawn outlines of women, men, mammoths, birds and animals. Often the human figures lie in a sort of frieze showing a procession or a dance. It is possible that 11,000 years ago, women danced on the banks of the Rhine as part of a religious ceremony.

There are many signs that the huts were lived in more than once. Some of the slates on the floor had one drawing on top of another and some of the heating stones had been replaced many times after they had sheltered in the heat of the fire. But it also seems likely that one of the huts was occupied only in winter and another only in summer. We know this from the animal bones. In the winter hut they belong to animals that were hunted in the cold season. The summer hut has many small hooves which shows that it was occupied in the months of warmer weather, the time when foals were born.

Flint remains help us to estimate where the two different groups came from. The winter dwellers used flint from quarries ninety-six kilometres to the north-west, so the people may have migrated to Gönnersdorf during the colder weather. The summer dwellers' flints could have come from no nearer than the river Meuse, over 100 kilometres to the west.

Did the two groups of people know each other? The remains on the site suggest that the summer and winter dwellers kept clear of each others' huts, though they may have lived alongside each other for a short while before one or other group moved on.

A reconstruction of how the Gönnersdorf huts may have been built. The excavators found holes for posts, and wedges which were used to hold the poles upright. The framework was probably left standing between visits to the site and re-covered each season.

The engravings on the paving stones on the hut floors included nearly 400 pictures of women and nearly 200 pictures of animals.

A sketch of life inside a Gönnersdorf hut, based on the objects found on the site. A large mammoth bone was used as a support on one side of the fire, which was kept alive by the draught from the hut opening. The woman has a special tool to lift one of the hot stones from the fire and put it into the hanging bowl to heat the liquid.

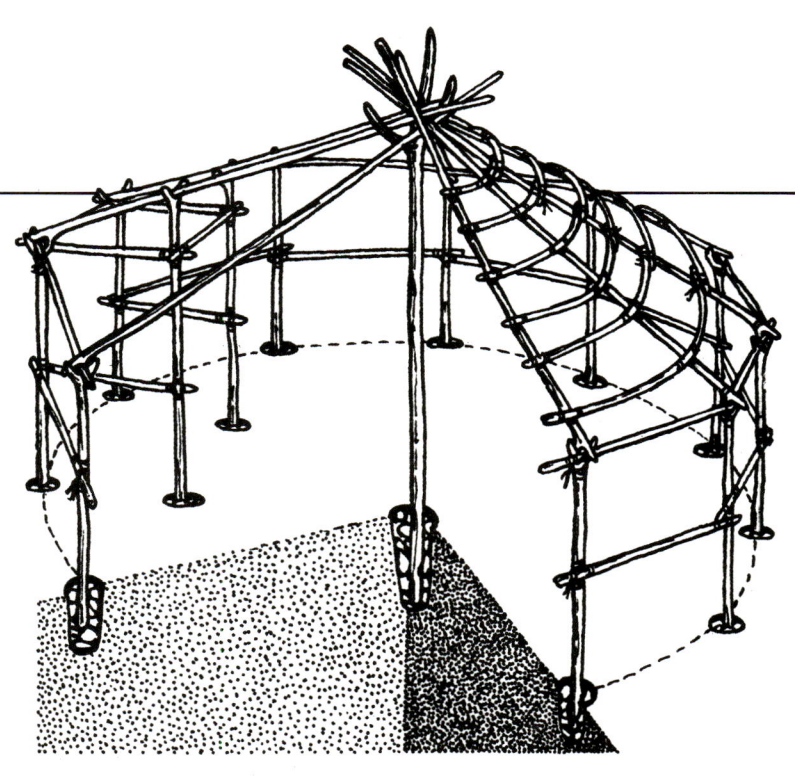

A reconstruction showing the hut covered with stitched horses' hides.

A NOMADIC LIFE

A common sight in Palaeolithic times must have been family groups travelling between two camps. Most Stone Age people had a nomadic way of life, but the sites at Pincevent and Gönnersdorf show that this did not mean they wandered about aimlessly. Their yearly travels took them from point to point according to the seasons, and they usually stayed in each place for a few weeks.

This is still the way of life of present-day hunter-gatherers such as the African Bushmen and Australian Aborigines. One family of Inuit in Alaska was studied for a year when they covered a 200-kilometre circuit, stopping eleven times. The complete tour crossed the basins of three rivers. When the movement of five families was studied over six years, it was seen that the circuits varied from year to year but that roughly the same amount of ground was covered.

Studies of prehistoric sites show that Palaeolithic people must have moved about in a similar way. In south-western Mexico, in the Tehuacan valley, there are 7,000-year-old sites which were occupied at different times in the year. Shelters have been found in the mountains where the people lived in winter, which was the dry period and the hunting season. In spring, they left these shelters to gather grain on the mountain slopes. In summer, they picked the fruit growing all over the valley then went back to their mountain camps when the dry season returned.

In Europe, we can piece together some of the Stone Age people's movements by flint remains. Sites (such as Gönnersdorf) often have flints which must have been carried for ninety kilometres or more. Part of the yearly journeying must have been to call in at good flint quarries. People often had to walk for many days to collect the kind of flint which they could not find locally. Such journeys in search of essential supplies became part of the regular pattern of life. Seashells were also moved around. In the Dordogne region of central France, excavators have found shells from the west coast and fossil shells from the north. People who visited Mas D'Azil in the Pyrenees between France and Spain wore ornaments of shells from both the Atlantic and the Mediterranean. Some people even ate sea fish a long way from the coast. Remains in a cave in the Gardon gorges in the south of France, almost fifty kilometres from the sea, show that the sea perch, a large fish, was eaten there.

Stone Age American Indians living between 10,000 and 8,000 BC were skilled at cutting obsidian, a rock which looks like bottle-glass. This spear tip is shown actual size.

This grooved spearhead, known as a Folsom point, was made by people of the American Folsom culture. The name 'Folsom' comes from remains found in New Mexico in the USA.

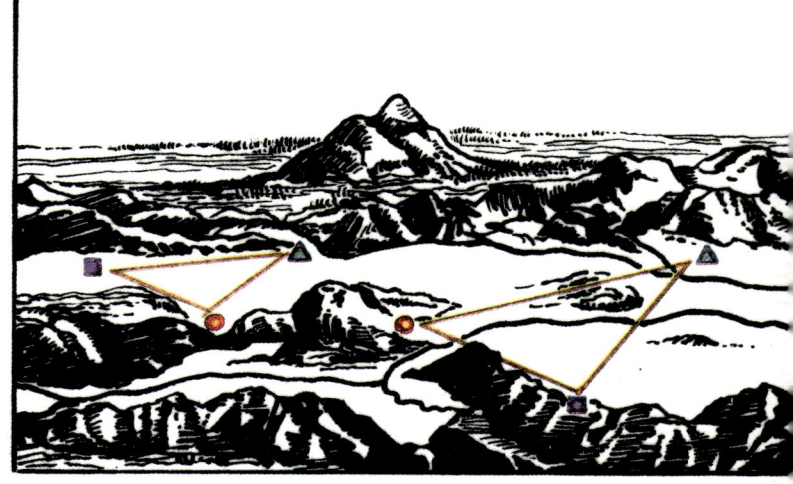

Stone Age hunter-gatherers on the move in the Tehuacan valley. Their travelling distances may have been shorter than those of many European people of Palaeolithic times.

A diagrammatic view of the Tehuacan valley which is about 30km long. Remains have been found of three different Stone Age groups who each had their own yearly circuit. The circles show their winter shelters. Triangles mark the areas where grain was gathered, and the squares mark the summer campsites.

THE REINDEER DEPART

The last Ice Age lasted for about 65,000 years. For all that time many parts of modern Europe, Asia and America would have been unrecognisable to us. Snow and ice covered the areas which today have mild climates. Towards the southern part of the ice sheets, some mosses grew and there may have been woodlands in sheltered corners. These were the grazing grounds of Europe's most common animal, the reindeer, and its huge rival, the mammoth.

The Ice Age reached its peak about 20,000 years ago. After that, the earth began to warm up very slowly. There were times when the ice crept south again, but mostly it retreated step by step. By about 9,000 BC the climate in Europe was mild. Forests grew and became homes for new animals such as the deer and the boar. The reindeer moved to the very north of Europe, where they could find the cold they were used to.

As the ice retreated, people began to move north, too. The best cave paintings of the Magdalenians come from the time when they were able to lead more settled lives on the northern slopes of the Pyrenees. In some places, the Magdalenian way of life lingered on for several centuries but it gradually gave way to a new culture, often called the Azilian culture because examples of their weapons and lifestyle were first found at Mas D'Azil in France. The Azilian way of life included hunting deer, wild oxen, boars and other small animals. The Azilians invented the first bow. The fine arrowheads and other new tools they made are said to belong to the Mesolithic or Middle Stone Age. The change in climate meant they could gather more of their food as berries, roots and edible plants.

People of the Azilian culture seem to have had no interest in cave painting or in carving bone and ivory. In most sites the only Azilian art found has been dots and lines scratched or painted on pebbles.

ARROWHEADS

The earliest arrowheads were found in woodland areas, where people of the Middle Stone Age lived after the last Ice Age. The blunt arrowheads may have been used for killing or stunning birds and other prey without breaking the skin.

New vegetation and new animals appeared after the last Ice Age. Hunting styles had to change. Bows and arrows appeared, as did spears with smaller blades. There was far more variety in the types of blade made and the work for which they could be used.

Harpoons used by Azilian hunters were made of bone or stag's horn. They were wide and flat, with a hole at the end for a thong.

In Denmark, at the same time, lived people who have been named Maglemonseans. Their harpoon tips had blades inserted down both sides of the bone.

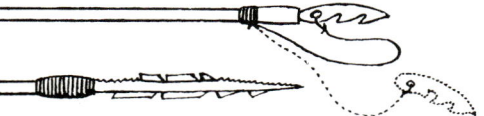

PEOPLE WHO LIVED BY THE SEA

After the glaciers disappeared, the groups of people who inhabited the world were almost all hunter-gatherers as their Ice Age ancestors had been. They hunted for some food and found the rest in the earth, on bushes or trees or in the water.

At Middle Stone Age sites near the coast, many piles of shells have been found. Sometimes these piles are several metres high and dozens of metres long. Some are made up of the remains of snails, while others consist of shellfish. They have been found on almost all the Atlantic coasts of Europe, North America, Brazil and North Africa.

Snails or shellfish must have played an important part in the lives of the people who made these piles of shells. But some groups were more daring. The remains of sea fish show that they were also active fishermen who sometimes went far out from land. Fishermen sailed to the Aegean islands from the mainland of Greece. From Europe they reached islands in the North Sea and the Atlantic. Several dugout canoes made from single tree trunks have been found. When one was uncovered in The Netherlands, it was over 8,000 years old. Another of about the same age was found in the river Seine in France. It is six metres long and may well have been used on the sea as well as in the river.

Like the forest people of Mesolithic times, those living on fish from rivers, lakes and the sea were beginning to settle down. Food was more plentiful and their hunting methods more skilful. For the first time it was possible to produce enough food without going on the yearly trek from site to site. The story of human beings was entering a new age....

MICROLITHS

A microlith is a tiny piece of stonework. Many Middle Stone Age people used implements which were hardly more than a centimetre long. They were made by breaking thin blades on an anvil into the shape needed.

A reconstruction of a Mesolithic site on the coast of Muge in Portugal. Traces of huts have been found here, as well as over a hundred graves with people buried in heaps of shells. Fish were caught at sea, and shellfish gathered along the shore. Sometimes a stranded whale would provide food, bone, skin and other materials. There are similar sites as far north as Denmark.

THE FIRST SETTLEMENTS

The last few pages have described some important changes in the centuries when the last Ice Age was slowly ending. People took more of their food from smaller animals and fish. They stayed longer in one campsite. Their tools and weapons became more varied with the coming of Mesolithic stone-workers.

Many of these changes happened first in lands at the eastern end of the Mediterranean Sea. This huge area stretches from central Turkey to Syria and Palestine, and across to Iran. In these countries archaeologists have found evidence of lifestyles which were quite different from the hunter-gathering ways of Old Stone Age peoples.

In many places, there are remains of small pits used to store grain from the seeds of wild grasses which grew locally. In the same sites, there are often fragments of pestles and mortars used for pounding and mixing food. Sometimes there are 'querns'. These were the stones used to grind grain to make a form of flour.

It is usual to find that most of the bones come from a single animal such as the gazelle, goat or sheep. Very often the bones are mostly of young animals. This suggests that the people of the settlement had half-domesticated the local wildlife by protecting them from beasts of prey. By eating a number of the young, the people kept the herds down to the number which could feed off the local wild foods. The animals did not therefore have to move on to new pastures.

These finds give us clues about a new stage in the development of human society. By about 11,000 BC some of the people in the Middle East were living in the first permanent settlements. Because they were able to store a year's supply of food, they were able to live in the same place all year round.

In Syria, the main animals were the gazelle and the aurochs – a kind of giant wild ox. The hunters may have tried to kill aurochs as a way of protecting the herds of gazelles. In a few places they may have taken the first steps towards domesticating the aurochs for its meat, hide and horns.

A reconstruction of a site at Mureybet in Syria in about 8,000 BC. The people had learned how to use the seeds of the best local grasses to grow their own grain crops in fields. Caring for the fields and pounding the grain with pestles and mortars was probably women's work. Animals were still not fully domesticated. The men hunted the beasts which preyed on the local herds of gazelle. Some gazelles were killed for food and for their skins, but killing was also a way of keeping down the numbers in each herd so that there was enough food in the area for all the animals.

HERDING IN THE ANDES

The Andes mountain range runs down the west coast of South America. In Peru the mountains rise to high plateaux which the local people call the Puna. Here there are vast areas of treeless land, thinly covered with grass. One of the peaks which looks out over the plateaux holds the rock shelter of Telamarchay, over 4,000 metres above sea level.

Telamarchay is the highest excavated prehistoric site in the world. There are another fifteen sites within a circle of about ten kilometres. Together these sites have helped archaeologists to trace an important stage in the story of human societies.

The first people came here 9,000 years ago as the earth warmed and grass began to grow on the Puna. The animal bones at the sites tell us that the people came as hunters and stayed at Telamarchay between December and April. One-third of their kills were deer. The other two-thirds were vicuna and guanaco, which are both animals from the camel family.

Two thousand years later, the bones tell a different story. Only one-fifth are from deer and nearly all the rest are from vicuna and guanaco. The minute remains of seeds and pollen show that the climate and plant life had not altered. The changes in the bones must therefore mean that the settlers were partly domesticating the vicuna and guanaco. That would have been fairly easy, as these animals will not stray if you mark the edges of their grazing grounds with a few stones. One of these stone boundaries has been found near one of the sites.

The people of Telamarchay were becoming herders as well as hunters and, as time went on, they became more skilled in their new way of life. Again the clues come from animal skeletons. In the fifth century BC, more and more of the teeth were exactly the same as those of the present-day alpaca. The alpaca comes from the same family as the vicuna and, like the llama, is kept for its wool. The herders must therefore have became stock-breeders. By choosing the best vicuna to breed, they gained new flocks of domesticated alpaca. Alpaca breeding provided the later prehistoric people at Telamarchay with the greatest share of their food.

The vicuna and guanaco, wild members of the camel family, still roam in the Andes. The mountain farmers tend the alpaca and the llama which are tame animals from the same family. *Top:* Vicuna as they might have been seen fleeing from hunters 10,000 years ago. *Bottom left:* Vicuna which have been partly domesticated. *Bottom right:* Present-day alpaca in the Puna.

EARLY FARMERS
THE FIRST HARVESTS

The skill of cultivating fields was almost certainly discovered by the women of prehistoric hunter-gathering times. As they gathered seeds and fruits, they must have noticed that grain spilled on the ground grew again the following year. They must have realised, too, that it grew best in certain places – where the ground was moist, for example, or where ashes had been spread.

Meanwhile, the men were finding that hunting was easier if they herded animals in certain places and that it was possible to increase the size of the herds by taking care not to kill mother beasts and protecting the young when they were born.

Once they had learned how to cultivate plants and breed animals, prehistoric peoples gave up the nomadic life and settled in one place. This happened in the Middle East around 8,000 BC. Sites from the time show that small, round mud huts were replaced by large, rectangular houses made of clay slabs fixed with mud and often divided into several rooms.

The remains of pollen at these sites show that the first cultivated crops were appearing. The settlers no longer plucked the seeds of wild grasses. They chose the ones which grew best, planted them, then harvested a cereal crop. In some places, cereals grew so successfully that the people gave up eating other food such as fish.

In western Europe, this new way of life came about more slowly because the land was covered with forests. Clearings had to be made by chopping down the trees and bushes, and burning them. Burning produced good crops because the heat cleared the soil of weeds and the ash fertilised it. But after a few years, the soil lost all its goodness and the people had to move on.

The people who followed the so-called 'slash and burn' way of farming used polished stone axes. This places them in what we call the Neolithic or New Stone Age. Gradually this gave way to the Bronze Age. Bronze is a mixture of copper and tin. Copper was the first metal to be used, when people discovered that it could be easily beaten into shapes. But between 3,000 and 2,000 BC, people in Europe discovered that a much harder metal could be made by blending copper and tin together. Bronze made sharper, tougher axes and knives, and it could also be used for the blade of a plough. With the coming of the Bronze Age, villagers no longer needed to move on when the soil was exhausted. Their fields were improved by ploughing and they could clear a large enough area to leave some fallow every few years. This gave the soil a chance to become fertile again.

Bronze Age pictures engraved on rock in the Camonica valley in the Italian Alps. They show bronze axes and daggers, and a plough drawn by oxen. The plough is a very simple one, with just a single blade to cut into the soil. The circular carvings may show a field enclosed with a fence, and another surrounded by ditches and a fence.

The first farmers stored their grain in large pottery jars. In Europe they used a quern to grind the grain into flour. A quern was a flat stone with a hollow in which the grain was crushed with a rounded stone.

The changes in farming occurred in the Middle East between 8,000 and 7,000 BC. An important new tool for these New Stone Age people was the sickle, which had a blade of polished stone fitted into a wooden handle. The woman in this picture is pounding grain with a heavy stone called a pestle in a large dish called a mortar. Pestles and mortars were used instead of querns in many parts of the Middle East. Notice the domesticated animals which were probably kept in a room in each house.

FARMING COMES TO MEXICO

The lands of the Middle East were only one of the areas of the world in which the way of life was based on farming. There were others in Asia (especially in north China) and in parts of Africa. The descendants of the people who had crossed from Asia into America also made their own changes from hunter-gathering to farming. One good example lies in the Tehuacan valley in Mexico.

On pages 30-31 we saw how the people of this valley hunted in winter and gathered grain in spring and fruit in summer. From around 7,000 BC this semi-nomadic way of life became more difficult. The climate was becoming warmer and the soil growing drier. Large animals could no longer live there, so the people had to find new ways of providing food. They began by choosing wild plants which they could develop into field crops. One was the avocado, and another was the gourd or squash.

In the next stage they began to grow beans, together with a new type of squash. There was also the calabash, a hard-skinned gourd which they did not eat but used as a container after they had scraped out the flesh. But the most important new crop was corn, even though at first the ears of this Indian corn were only a few centimetres long! It was as important in America as wheat was in the Middle East and Europe, and rice was in Asia.

Along with these new food crops came new utensils. As in the Middle East, the people of the Tehuacan valley began to make grinding stones and pestles and mortars.

At this stage these early farmers had not settled in one place for the whole year. They still lived in small groups which came together in spring to plant the corn. The final stage of the change from hunter-gatherers to farmers came when they built the first permanent villages in the heart of the valley. There were usually between five and ten huts as well as larger shelters, and trenches for storing food. The people of these settlements began to grow a wider variety of crops, with new kinds of bean and corn and possibly pumpkins.

The people of the Tehuacan valley now had permanent villages, but the remains show that their diet still included some wild plants and animals until about 2,500 BC. The change to a way of life where they grew all their own food had taken almost 5,000 years.

At about this time, the first pottery appeared. It was crudely made and contained pieces of grit in the clay. The skill was probably learned from other people in South America who had been making pottery for some time.

Corn

Runner beans

Sweet potato

Vanilla

Between 7,000 and 1,500 BC the people of Mexico domesticated many plants which are part of today's diet. Many of them were grown only in the Americas until very recent times.

Peanut

Avocado

Brazilian squash

Cotton

Papaya

Tomato

Prickly pear

Cocoa beans

Manioc roots

THE FIRST GODS

Cave paintings, statuettes and other works of art show that Stone Age people held some magical or religious beliefs almost from the time that *Homo sapiens* first appeared. They painted and carved animals and used magical signs to help hunting or new birth in spring. The hunter-gatherers and fishers of Syria and Palestine in the Middle East made small figures, too. Only a few examples have survived. Eleven of them represent gazelles, which were the most frequently hunted animals. These figures were used in ceremonies connected with hunting, but this is not the same as making figures of gods which are worshipped for their great powers.

People seem to have begun to develop a belief in gods and goddesses around 9,000 BC. In the Middle Eastern sites of this time, small stone or clay figures have been found. Almost all are models of women with very wide hips. Over the next thousand years or so, these tiny models were replaced by larger statuettes. Some have very wide hips which are out of proportion to their small heads. Others have large heads. The eyes were made bigger and bigger as time went on, and the statues came to look less and less like real women. It seems that they were made as symbols of powers which were more than human.

At Çatal Hüyük in Turkey there are many examples of an enormously fat female figure. Sometimes she was carved giving birth, seated between two panthers. She was also shown in a plaster wall modelling, giving birth to bulls. In the same rooms there were plaster bulls' heads and horns. It seems that the people of this site had come to believe in two great gods. One was the Great Mother Goddess, who gave birth to men and animals and was responsible for all creation. The other was her mate, the Bull-God, who represented all the power and majesty of the heavens.

These figures are often taken to mark the beginning of human belief in gods among the people of Europe and the Middle East. The Great Mother Goddess and the Bull-God appear in many ancient myths and beliefs about gods and the creation of world. In Mesopotamia, along the banks of the Tigris and the Euphrates rivers, people believed in the Bull of Heaven. The early Egyptians worshipped the cow-goddess, Hathor. Ancient Greek myths tell the story of Europa, a king's daughter who was carried away by the god Zeus in the form of a bull so that they could have three sons.

The societies who created the images of gods in human and animal form soon found the need to have people to act as interpreters of the gods' will. This need led to the appearance of the first priests and priestesses.

Statuettes of female figures like this were made in the Cyclades islands near Greece between 4,000 and 3,000 BC. They represent a stage on the way to models of goddesses.

One of the figures of a great fish-god which have been found in New Stone Age settlements on the banks of the river Danube. It seems natural that the people who lived near this wide river believed in the powers of gods whose home was in the water and who created their main supply of food.

The Great Mother Goddess of Çatal Hüyük seated between two panthers.

A figure from another part of the Middle East, showing a life-giving goddess. Her huge body is covered with symbolic marks.

CANOES ON THE MEDITERRANEAN

The first cultivated crops were harvested in the Middle East about 10,000 years ago. It was another 2,000 years before the first signs of this new way of life were seen on the shores of Italy, Spain, France and Morocco in the western Mediterranean.

Some time before 6,000 BC, small groups of people from the eastern Mediterranean packed their tools, pottery and a few young animals into dugout canoes and set out to sea. They landed at different places along the western Mediterranean coasts, and there they settled. Shortly afterwards some left these sites and moved even further west. After hundreds of years there were settlements on the shores of all the countries along the western Mediterranean.

When archaeologists uncover these western Mediterranean sites they usually find remains of 'impressed-ware' pottery, so-called because the potters used cockle shells to press a crinkly pattern into the clay before it was fired. Sometimes this pottery is known as 'cardial', from the Latin name for the cockle – *Cardium edule*. The oldest cardial pottery comes from the eastern Mediterranean. Stage by stage, seagoing travellers brought it to the western shores.

Alongside the pottery remains are often the bones of domesticated goats and sheep. There are also querns and pestles and mortars, but these were usually used to grind wild grains. It seems that these first newcomers brought the skill of herding animals but did not cultivate their own fields. Perhaps there were too few people to carry out all the work.

A few hundred years later, new settlers began to arrive with the seed corn of wheat and barley. This was one of the beginnings of what is sometimes called the Neolithic Revolution in western Europe, when the archaeologists can show us that people using polished stone axes and knives began to build villages and cultivate the surrounding fields. These newcomers found fertile valleys only a few days' walk from the sea, where they could build their small settlements of round huts faced with stones.

It is still impossible to know whether Neolithic farming came to western Europe only through the skill and knowledge of newcomers from the east, but the discovery of inland sites in France and Spain where people were beginning to grow crops, make pottery and care for some animals suggests that farming would soon have developed in western Europe without the help of newcomers from lands where it had been practised for about 2,000 years.

An 'impressed-ware' pot found near Alicante in Spain. It is just over 20cm high and shows how the cockle shells were used to make the decorations.

A family coming to settle in a new home. They are carrying tools, pots and some young animals. They may have come only a short distance from a settlement to the east. Later, when the family has grown, some of its members might move on to a new site further west.

The first animal to be domesticated seems to have been the dog. Next were the sheep and the goat, which looked very similar in Neolithic times. As well as keeping flocks, Neolithic people were also hunters. They used bows and arrows fitted with polished stone points.

In the background is a round, wooden hut, thatched with leaves or grass and faced with stone.

DANUBIAN LONGHOUSES

Between 5,000 and 4,000 BC, another wave of movement and settlement brought farming to central and northern Europe. It began on the banks of the river Danube in modern Hungary and Czechoslovakia. People living here by about 5,000 BC had learned how to clear forests to plant wheat and graze their pigs, cattle and sheep.

Farming on the banks of the Danube was so successful that the size of settlements grew. One settlement often contained more than a hundred people. Their homes were longhouses, all built to almost exactly the same pattern. The walls were made from posts covered with wattle (a woven layer of twigs and soft branches). The wattle was then plastered with clay mud. The steep roof was held up by timbers supported by lines of posts inside the house. It was usually thatched with reeds on a wooden framework. The very first houses were rectangular in shape, but they soon became broader at the end where the door was. The door always faced away from the winds which blew across Europe from the Atlantic Ocean. Outside, there was always a ditch. The clay for the walls was dug from this and the hole that was left behind became a refuse heap, or midden', where rubbish was thrown.

Like other early people who cleared forests, the Danubians found that the soil in their fields became less fertile after a few years. Then they had to move on to clear another area. Some made new settlements nearby, but the population was growing so fast that others had to push further west or north-west. After a few centuries, there were Danubian people across most of Germany, The Netherlands, Belgium and the north-west of France. Danubian sites have been found in all these countries. All that remains of their homes are the post-holes which confirm that all longhouses were built to the same pattern and always faced the same direction away from the winds.

A reconstruction of a Danubian longhouse. Each house had one large room, with a porch at the door end. Some longhouses were up to 36m long. They have been found with only one hearth and with several, which may tell us the number of families who shared the house. The homes in a settlement were built close to each other.

In the bottom part of the picture is an 'incised' or 'ribbon' pot, so-called because of the way in which the ribbon-like pattern was cut, or incised, into the clay. You can also see a piece of wattle, and rushes ready to be used for thatch. Danubians kept cattle and pigs, which were closely related to wild boar.

THE HOUSES OF LES FONTINETTES

An aerial view of the post-holes and ditches of longhouses at Les Fontinettes in the valley of the river Aisne in France. These were the homes of some of the first farmers in northern Europe.

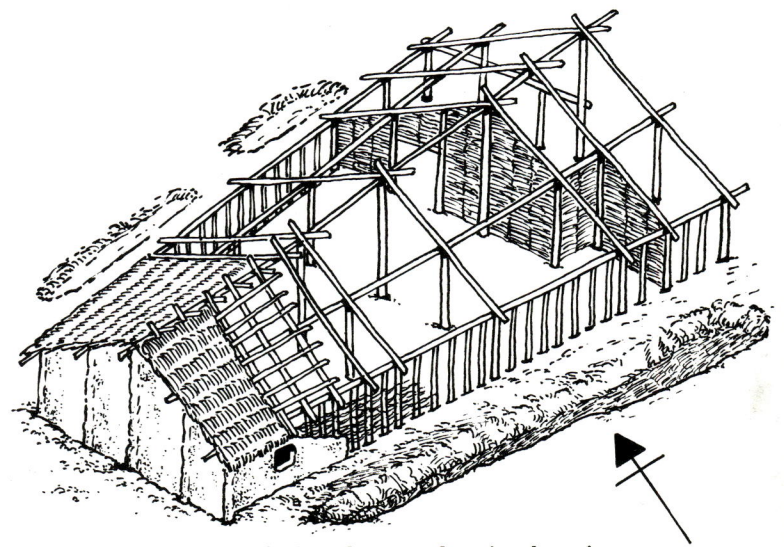

A plan of a longhouse, showing how it broadened at the door end and how the roof and walls were built. Clay came from the surrounding ditches.

MEGALITHIC TOMB-BUILDERS

Only a few centuries after farming came to western Europe, people began to build megalithic monuments. The word megalithic comes from two Greek words meaning 'large stone'.

Megalithic monuments can be found all over the world, and there are thousands in western Europe. The oldest are found in Spain, Portugal and France. They date back to nearly 5,000 BC, 2,000 years before the pyramids were built in Egypt. By 3,000 BC megaliths had spread to north Germany, Denmark, Norway, Ireland and Britain, as far as the remote islands north of Scotland.

Most of the megaliths were tombs. The huge stones were set up to make passageways leading to burial chambers. Sometimes there was just one chamber and one passageway, but the largest tombs may have had several. After the stonework was finished, the whole tomb was covered with a mound of earth called a tumulus. This mound is often all that can be seen today.

Some tombs were turned into monuments by putting a stone building instead of an earth tumulus above them. These would have been visible across a large area, just as church towers are today.

Hundreds of people were needed to cut and move the stones for megalithic tombs. They must have come from many settlements and someone, perhaps a chief or a priest, must have organised the work, all of which was done by human muscle power without the help of animals. Most burial chambers contain only a few skeletons, and it seems likely that they were the tombs of those same chiefs or priests who planned them and supervised the work.

A megalithic tomb with the tumulus cleared away to show the way in which the passage and burial chamber were built.

One of the megalithic tombs at Bougon, Deux-Sèvres, in France. Instead of an earth tumulus, this tomb has been covered with small stones.

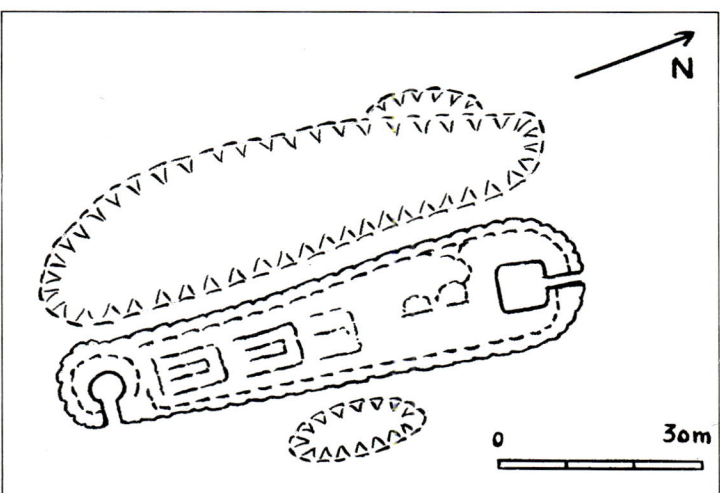

A plan of another tumulus at Bougon. It shows two burial chambers, one at each end, one round and the other square. They date from different periods. The sketches above and below the tumulus show the quarries from which the stones were taken.

0   30m

How do you carry a stone which weighs 30 tonnes? Experiments were carried out at Bougon which showed that it can be done with 200 men, some ropes, some tree trunks, levers made of oak – and plenty of time!

PEOPLES OF THE GREEN SAHARA

The Sahara, in Africa, is the largest desert in the world. Nine thousand years ago it was a huge area of grassland with many rivers and lakes. Elephants, rhinoceroses and antelopes roamed across the land. The waters held hippopotamuses, crocodiles and many fish.

There were people, too, in the Sahara. One group lived among the rocks at Amekni, on the western slopes of the Ahaggar mountains. Excavations tell us that they built shelters of fig-tree branches roofed with skins or woven mats. They hunted buffalo and antelope, and trapped fish by building dams in the rivers. They were also cattle herders. Remains in caves show that they moved their herds from the plains to mountain pastures each season. They harvested a cereal called millet, which they stored in large pottery jars. Long before pottery existed in the Middle East it seems to have been in daily use in the Sahara.

North-east of the Ahagger mountains other prehistoric people lived in the Tassili district. As well as being hunter-gatherers and skilled potters like the people at Amekni, the Tassili people were also fine artists and made hundreds of rock paintings.

But the Saharan climate soon started to change. The rainfall lessened, and the grasslands became dry and parched. It was no longer possible to kill and collect enough food from one place. The Saharan people turned to herding cattle, and wandering with them from one patch of fertile ground to the next. By about 2,500 BC the Sahara was becoming too dry for even this way of life. Its people moved away, some to the shores of the Mediterranean, some to the grasslands and forests of West Africa and some to the settlements that were growing along the river Nile.

A reconstruction of a scene in the central Sahara. People are taking their cattle to a new grazing land.

A Tassili rock painting showing bowmen with a herd of cattle. It may be a hunting scene, or the bowmen may be defending their herds and themselves from attack.

THE PAINTINGS OF TASSILI

The hundreds of rock paintings at Tassili illustrate the daily life of the people in about 4,000 BC, when the Sahara was green and supported a way of life which was more advanced than that in most other parts of the world.

SAHARA

TASSILI

AHAGGAR MOUNTAINS

LAKE VILLAGES

At the time the Danubian people were erecting their long-houses in northern Europe, the people of western Europe were building their megalithic monuments and the settlers on the shores of the Mediterranean were imitating methods of farming which came from the Middle East, yet another type of settlement was developing in the centre of the continent. In the Alps and in the Jura mountains of Switzerland, as well as in the nearby parts of Italy, Germany and France, people were beginning to build villages on the shores of lakes. Some villages were even built over the water itself.

Many of these villages have been excavated so that we can study the similarities and differences between them. The houses were nearly always rectangular, but there were many different ways of stopping them from sinking. Some were built on log rafts so that the whole village floated. In other places, the builders sank wooden posts very deep into the marshy ground or into the earth below the lake waters.

Because the wooden posts were in water, they often continued to grow. This new growth was shown by the formation of a new ring in the wood each year, similar to the rings seen on tree trunks. This means that it is possible to work out how long a house stood before it was abandoned or had to be repaired. On Lake Wauwil in Switzerland, for example, seven houses were built around 3,000 BC. They had to be repaired after six years, and between twelve and fifteen years later the people left for good. Near Grenoble in France a site was lived in for about thirty years and then abandoned for between thirty and forty years. After that it was occupied again for another thirty years. The posts in a bog village in the north of Switzerland tell a different story. There were eleven large houses that could shelter thirty families. People lived in them for over a century. During those years the floor level of one of the houses had to be raised eleven times!

Many lake village sites lie under water today. The water has preserved a number of objects. Here you can see the remains of the wooden posts on which houses were built.

A lake village scene. The houses are built close together, without any farming land. The villagers' main food was fish, which they caught with harpoons and in nets.

WOODWORKING

The excavations at lake village sites have produced many objects preserved by the water. If they had been on land these objects would have decayed into dust. From them we know that prehistoric times were not just stone ages. They were also ages of wood.

The lake villagers were Neolithic people who made axes, knives, harpoon points and arrowheads out of polished stone. But, of course, they fitted them into wooden handles of different sizes and shapes. They learned that ash is the best wood for an axe handle because it is both tough and springy. Fitting the blade into the ash was a difficult problem. The lake villagers' solution was to fix a socket made from a stag's horn on to the handle and set the blade in this. House builders discovered how to split the trunks of oak and ash trees by driving in wedges of hard beechwood. They also developed special joints to hold the posts together. These joints allowed them to build stronger, lighter house frameworks.

For knives, the lake villagers fitted flint blades into grooves cut into whitewood handles. The hilts of daggers were made of yew, ash, willow or bone. For arrow shafts they chose long, thin branches of hazel, elm or ash. Bows were made of yew, although one longbow of ashwood has been found, almost two metres in length. Some people carried clubs or throwing weapons which look like boomerangs. At other times they used javelins of poplar, willow and hazelwood, and lances of ash or yew.

Woodworkers took the knobbly growths on tree trunks and carved them into bowls, cups and ladles. They made plates and spoons from pieces of maple, ash and poplar. Bark was used to make the sides of containers, built up from a wooden base. Inside bark there is a layer of fibres through which the sap rises. The fibres were stripped away and spun into rope and string. With these the lake people made fishing nets, baskets and mats.

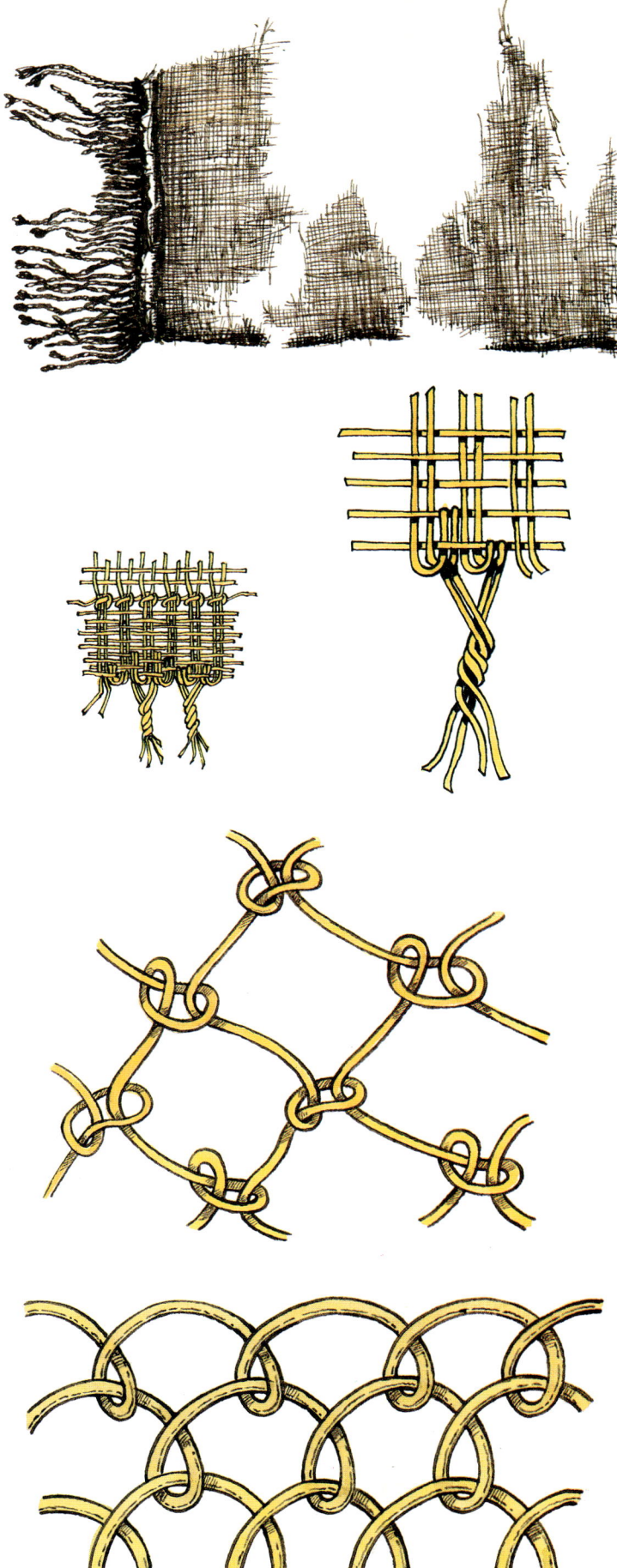

Many different types of wooden combs have been found in the sites of lake villages. Each district seems to have had its own fashion.

Four wooden objects found in lake village sites.
Left: A dagger with a flint blade fitted into a wooden hilt, lashed with willow twigs.
Centre top: A knife with a flint blade fitted into a short wooden socket.
Centre bottom: A ladle.
Right: A maplewood cup.

◁ Fragments of woven materials have been preserved.
Top: A piece of material with a hem and black fringe, found near Zurich.
Centre: The finds have helped experts to see how weaving was done.
Bottom: Two examples of the knots used to make fishing nets.

Necklaces, like this one, were usually made of bones and teeth.

FORTIFIED CAMPS

While some people were building their lake villages, another type of settlement was appearing across Europe from Poland to Britain. These were camps built on high ground and surrounded by a ring of fortifications. Usually, the builders dug two or three ditches and used the earth to make embankments.

Sometimes Neolithic people built houses for themselves and their animals inside the ring of ditches. In the daytime, many of them went to work in the surrounding fields. Others took the cattle and sheep out of the settlement and watched over them while they grazed. In other sites there are few remains of buildings inside the fortifications. It is likely that people lived nearby and built the camp as a place they could retreat to. One of these camps without buildings is at Windmill Hill in southern England, which dates from about 3,000 BC. Here the signs of settlement are outside the camp and in the spaces between the ditches.

In France a camp with two ditches was built at Berry-au-Bac about 3,600 BC. The post-holes show that there were no more than four square or rectangular houses inside the ditches. At Noyen in the Seine valley another camp has an inside area which was once four hectares and may have been increased to twelve hectares.

It may be that some of these camps, like Windmill Hill, were built as places where Neolithic people could meet to exchange goods. Or they might have been used as meeting places for all the villagers from one tribe.

The way into a camp was by one of the causeways across the ditches. At Windmill Hill and at many other sites there are so many causeways that the camp would have been very hard to defend. In a few other sites, however, there are signs of defences. The causeways were built so that enemies would have to go round corners to get into the central area. There were also towers and barriers at some of the entrances. Sometimes one side of the camp was protected by a steep cliff. This meant that the builders had to put up their ditches and embankments only on the sides where the ground was more level. In some lakeside settlements the water formed part of the defences, with a stout wooden stockade on the side facing dry land. In at least one case the settlers surrounded themselves with clear water by building their lake village sixty metres from the shore.

Why did New Stone Age people build fortified camps? In some parts of Europe the camps may tell us that the population was growing and that land was becoming scarce. Different groups of farmers may have begun to fight over the best places to grow their crops and graze their animals. A group with a fortified camp would have appeared much more powerful than neighbours who did not have enough people or the right sort of skills to build one.

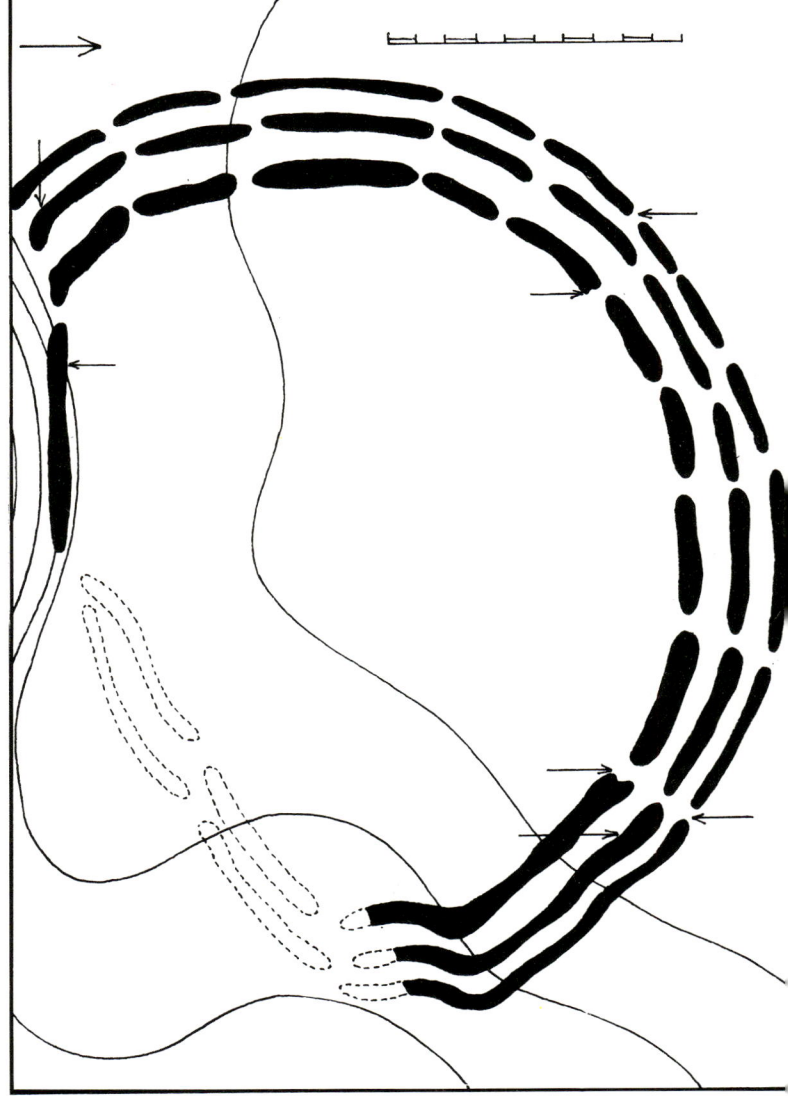

Champ Durand, a fortified camp in the west of France.
Left: A plan.
Right: A reconstruction based on finds at the site.
The contour lines on the plan show that the land was steep on the left. The more level sides were protected by three lines of ditches and earthworks. The positions of the tower and causeway entrances in the picture have been based on remains found at the site.

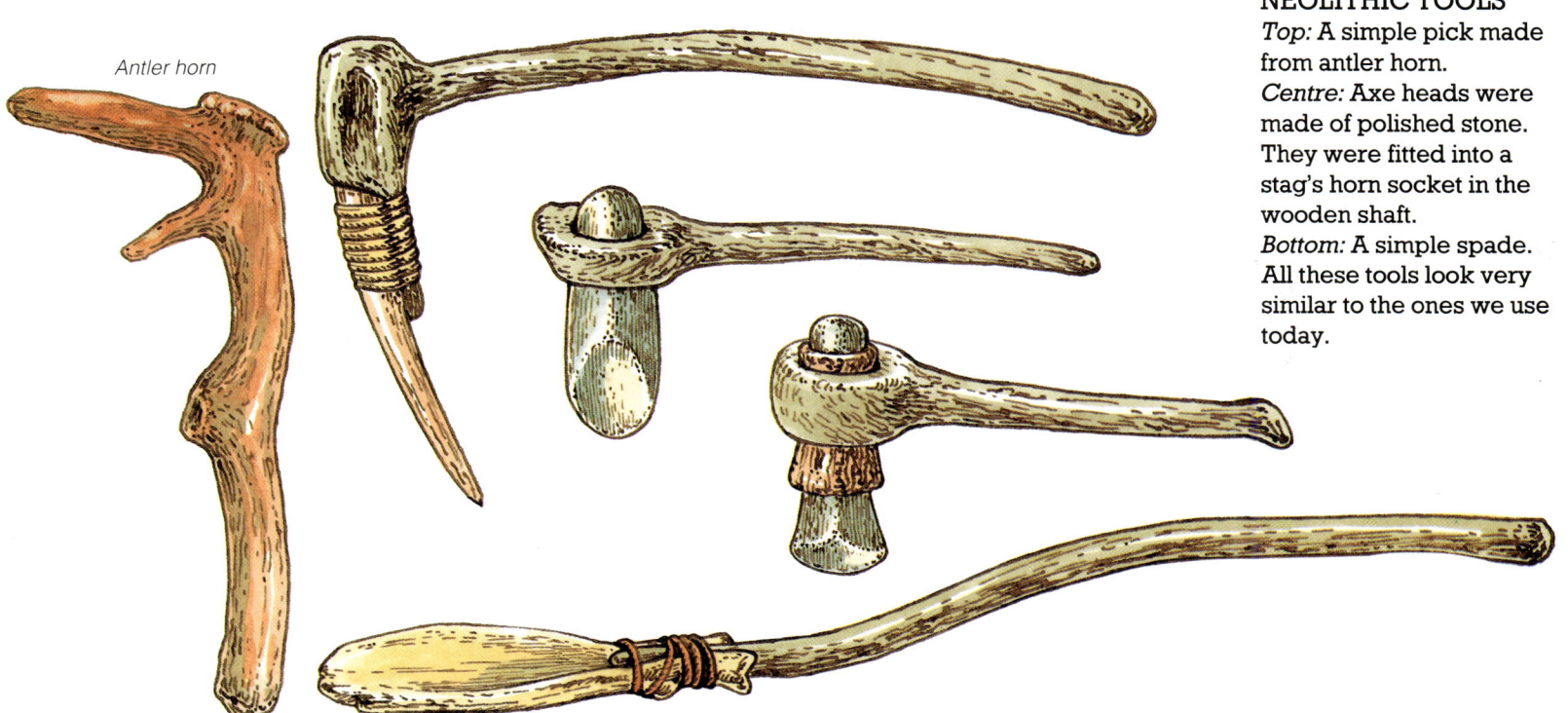

NEOLITHIC TOOLS

Top: A simple pick made from antler horn.

Centre: Axe heads were made of polished stone. They were fitted into a stag's horn socket in the wooden shaft.

Bottom: A simple spade. All these tools look very similar to the ones we use today.

Antler horn

STONEHENGE

Stonehenge is a colossal monument on Salisbury Plain in southern England. The first work was done by Neolithic people around 2,300 BC. About 1,000 years later, Bronze Age builders made Stonehenge even more massive.

The first Neolithic work was a circular ditch and earth bank which enclosed a space almost ninety-eight metres across. A huge stone, known as the heelstone, was set up outside the ditch to the north-east, just at the point where the sun rises on Midsummer's Day. About 400 years later, other Neolithic people put two circles of bluestones, each with thirty blocks, in the centre of the enclosure. Some of these stones may have been used for tracking the position of the sun and moon.

Somewhere between 1,700 and 1,350 BC, Bronze Age people took down the bluestone circles. In their place they put up a single circle of thirty sarsens (blocks of sandstone) which they joined at the top with lintels made of other massive stones. Inside this ring they put up five trilothons. A trilothon is a set of three stones with two uprights and one lintel joining them across the top. The trilothons were laid out in a horseshoe shape, and inside them was put another horseshoe of nineteen bluestones.

Stonehenge shows that the Neolithic and Bronze Age peoples had wonderful building skills. It has been calculated that it would have taken 250 men to set the thirty-five-tonne heelstone upright. The bluestones were brought 560 kilometres from mountains in Wales. The sarsens came from Marlborough Down, only thirty-two kilometres away, but they weigh fifty tonnes each and would have needed 1,500 men to move them and set them up.

No one knows why Stonehenge was built, but it may have been some kind of observatory to help in working out the calendar. It may also have been a temple.

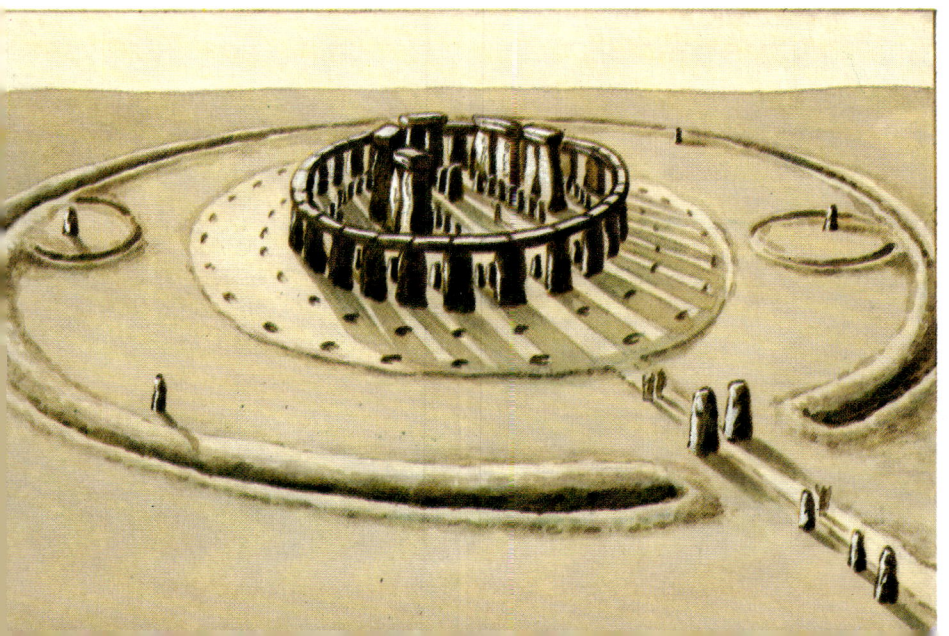

Stonehenge as it must have looked around 1,550 BC, when the last important work was finished. The avenue approaching it pointed towards sunrise on Midsummer's Day.

Neolithic and Bronze Age people made nothing quite like Stonehenge anywhere else in Europe.

Each 50-tonne sarsen was pulled to Stonehenge on rollers. But how did Bronze Age builders set them upright and then place others which were nearly as heavy on top? The diagrams below show how archaeologists think it was done.
Top row: The sarsen was placed on the edge of a pit and levered until it tipped in. Then it was pulled upright by men hauling on ropes while others put wooden supports behind.
Bottom row: The lintel was levered up stage by stage on a wooden platform which was built higher after each lift.

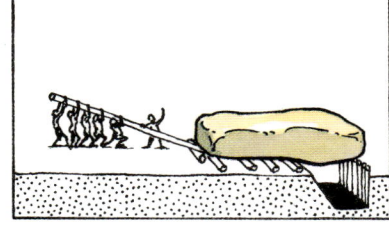  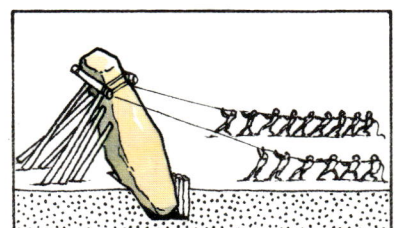 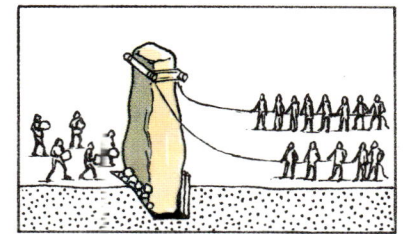

RED METAL

When prehistoric people discovered a new method of making something, they often first used it to make jewellery. It might be hundreds of years before the new method was used to help hunting, farming or daily life. The first people to polish stone, for example, made pendants and bracelets long before they made stone axe heads. Potters made small figures and statuettes before their great-great-grandchildren made cooking pots. It was the same with the first metals.

The earliest metal workers we know of lived in eastern Turkey between 7,000 and 6,000 BC. They prised small pieces of copper out of the rock and hammered it into small beads and pins. After 4,000 BC, copper workers in Iran learnt how to heat the rock, or ore, in which the copper was found until the copper turned into liquid and ran out of the rock. This happens when the ore is heated to 927°C. This pure, liquid copper could be poured into moulds in the shapes of axes, hoes, chisels and awls, which were used for boring.

At about the same time, some people in the south-east of Europe also found out how to 'smelt' copper, as this process was known, and make useful tools. From there, the skill spread to western Europe. Around 2,800 BC, some lake dwellers in Switzerland were able to smelt. In one site, two strings of copper beads have been found which may have been used as an early form of money. Copper awls have also been found in the passageways of some of the Megalith tombs in Spain.

Very often working in copper and gold went together. People found grains of gold in river beds and discovered that they could be hammered together and shaped into ornaments using the same tools and skills as were used for copper.

A favourite form of decoration made by Bronze Age goldsmiths were necklets and circular collars. Many of the best examples have been found in Ireland.

GOLD IN THE BRONZE AGE

Gold was often used in the Bronze Age. Many goldsmiths decorated their work with geometric designs like those on this gold cup, which comes from the Museum of National Antiquities at St Germain-en-Laye in France.

People gather round a traveller who has brought some glittering metal beads from far away. In many parts of the world copper and metal ornaments were worn for hundreds and thousands of years before metal was used for everyday objects.

THE BRONZE AGE

Making objects out of bronze followed naturally from skill in copper-working. After 4,000 BC, coppersmiths in many parts of the Middle East and some of the lands and islands in the eastern Mediterranean learnt how to smelt copper ore to obtain pure copper. They then discovered that they could make a much harder metal if they smelted some tin with the copper.

When the red-hot liquid metal had separated from the ore, the bronzesmith could do two things. He could let the bronze cool into blocks or bars which could be beaten into sheets to make helmets, armour or ornaments, or he could let it run into moulds so that when it cooled it was an axe head, a dagger or some other solid object. This second method of working is known as casting.

Bronzesmiths' workplaces needed a lot of equipment and many assistants. Some smelted the copper and tin, others made moulds for casting, others beat sheets of metal so that still others could cut and bend these into the shapes they needed. Objects such as helmets were then reheated so the edges could be joined, or welded together. Because of the special equipment and skills, bronze-working could not be done in every settlement. Instead, a few specialist centres grew up and traders carried the objects they made to sell or barter perhaps far away.

In Europe the earliest bronze-making centres were in the south of modern Germany, Czechoslovakia, and Hungary. The skill spread to centres in southern Spain and to parts of Wales, Scotland and Ireland. The tin used by the bronze-smiths often came from far away. One of the busiest places for tin mining was in Cornwall, and Cornish tin made its way all over Europe.

A Bronze Age helmet, showing where it was welded together. Other items of bronze armour were breastplates and leg protectors.

An axe head, and the two halves of the mould in which it was cast. The liquid metal was poured through the top when the two halves were together.

A Bronze Age chieftain and a bronzesmith. The chieftain is wearing bronze ornaments made in styles which were common in western Europe. He carries a bronze dagger. The smith is showing a sword he has just made. It has two notches between the handle and the blade to give a better grip. Many of these swords have been found and it is likely that thousands were made in this style.

THE IRON AGE

In the Jura mountains of Switzerland traces have been found of people who lived towards the very end of the Bronze Age, around 1,000 BC. They occupied the same caves seven times in a hundred years. Each time the numbers in the caves were smaller. The caves acted as a hiding place, as bands of warriors launched attack after attack on their settlements.

The raiders were Celts, related to people who settled around the river Danube. It was not long before the Celts became the most powerful group in central Europe. Behind their power lay their skill in using a new metal, iron. The Celts also used horses, which they hitched to war chariots and carts with the help of harness made of leather and iron. The Celts spread west to France, Spain, western Germany, Britain and Ireland, and for many centuries Celtic people and Celtic languages dominated the way of life in all those countries.

Celts organised themselves in a more complex way than earlier farming peoples. Each group had its chief and a number of powerful warriors. The centre of a Celtic community was usually a hilltop fort. Here the chief and the warriors lived, along with priests and craft workers such as smiths, potters and weavers. Around the hillfort were the farms of the ordinary people who tilled their fields with the help of ploughs. The Celts were the first people to use ploughs on a large scale.

Just as the Celts brought iron, the horse and the plough to western Europe, other peoples took these discoveries to other regions. Scythians moved into the southern Soviet Union and their warriors, traders and craftsmen became overlords of the people already living there. In the Middle East the Medes and the Persians set up great empires.

In Europe the power of the Celts was overtaken by a growing empire which had its headquarters in Rome. In the first century BC, Roman armies conquered most of the Celtic people in western Europe and in the first century AD they added Britain to their empire. Even so, the Celtic language and way of life lasted for many years among village people, and the Romans never destroyed it in Ireland, Wales or Scotland.

The sword was the weapon which made it possible for first Bronze Age and then Iron Age people to become masters of vast areas. At the very beginning of the Iron Age, iron was scarce and was used only to decorate bronze weapons.

The Celts spread quickly into the
countries of western Europe. As they
approached, the people already living
there tried to protect themselves by
building stockades round their
settlements, but this was not enough to
stop the raiders. After the Celts had
overrun a settlement, the people merged
their way of life with that of the
newcomers.

THE STORY OF PREHISTORIC STUDIES

In the eighteenth century, no one believed that there had been a long period of pre-history before early civilisations began. Scholars used the Bible's story of the creation of the world and the coming of the first people, Adam and Eve, to work out that the earth had begun only 6,000 years before. Many people had seen flint tools and believed they had been used by early people who they thought must have lived like some of the 'savages' described by explorers. But they had no idea of the great length of time the Stone Ages had lasted or of the many steps by which human-type creatures developed into modern human beings.

Rocks and fossils

In the nineteenth century, geology began to change scholars' views of the origins of the earth and the life on it. Geology is the study of rocks and how they were formed, and geologists soon realised that there were two main groups. Some rocks were igneous, which means they were formed by the great heat of a volcano. Others were sedimentary, which means they were layers of mud, sand or plant life which had lain under great pressure for a very long time until they became slate, sandstone or coal. Once they knew how these rocks were made, geologists tried to calculate how long it had taken. A French geologist worked out that the earth must be over 2 million years old. He dared not publish this calculation for fear of being mocked or attacked by people who believed in the truth of the Bible. So he announced that the earth was 75,000 years old – but he was criticised by other scholars even for saying this!

Paleontologists played a part in changing ideas about the age of the earth. They are students of fossils (the remains of prehistoric animals or plants), which can be found in many very old rocks. Paleontologists began to realise that the earth must have gone through many upheavals to reach its present shape when they found fossils of sea and mud

In the middle of the nineteenth century many artists were inspired by stories of the discovery of remains of prehistoric settlements. One made this engraving of 'Man from the lakeside settlements'.

creatures in rocks in some mountains. A French paleontologist, Georges Cuvier, studied fossils on the Greek island of Crete to see if they could be made to fit with the story of creation in Genesis, the first book of the Old Testament, which tells how the earth was made in six days. He suggested that the fossils showed that there must have been four creations which were each destroyed by great upheavals before the fifth, when humans and present-day animals were created.

Georges Cuvier's ideas did not fit with the fact that the bones of early humans and human-type creatures were often found alongside the bones of extinct animals. In 1858, an English geologist, Hugh Falconer, went to see the collection of Jacques Boucher de Perthes. Perthes was a French customs officer who had collected stone tools from sites which also contained mammoth bones. Hugh Falconer sent for other English geolo-

In 1903, the French artist, Paul Jamin, painted this picture called 'Decorative painter of the Stone Age'. The details of how people lived and dressed came from his imagination.

gists who agreed with him that the bones were proof people existed long before the coming of any kind of civilisation.

The age of Charles Darwin

One man who studied the work of geologists and paleontologists was the English scientist, Charles Darwin. In 1859 he published his book *On the Origin of Species*. Darwin had no doubt that all animal and plant life had gone through many stages of evolution before reaching their present state. He also believed that all living things had developed from the first simple creatures living in the seas. Some had died out, but others had changed their form just enough to survive through changes in the shape of the earth or in its climate and food supply. This evolution had gone on step by step over millions of years.

On the Origin of Species was a sensation when it was published because of Darwin's view that humans must have developed from some kind of ape, the creature in the animal kingdom most similar to humans. Some supporters of Darwin believed that one day a 'missing link' between apes and humans would be found.

The first possible missing link had been the skeletons found in the Neander valley in Germany in 1858. At first, people argued that this 'Neanderthal Man' was some kind of monster or a cripple. But other Neanderthal remains were found in Belgium and in Gibraltar, and it had to be recognised that another kind of human being had existed before the modern human.

The search went on for the missing link, or *Pithecanthropus*, which is Greek for ape-man. In 1891 a Dutch doctor, Eugene Dubois, discovered 'Java Man' on the island of Java in Indonesia. Java Man's skull was very flat-topped, with a heavy ridge of bones above the eyes. It was not the skull of an ape but it was not a human skull either. Gradually, other examples of *Pithecanthropus* were discovered. 'Peking Man' was discovered in north China. Near Johannesburg in South Africa there was the Taung skull, found in 1924. It belonged to a creature

The sculptor Emile Derré was photographed about 1910 with a sculpture he called 'Prehistoric Man'. The idea obviously came from finds of scientists looking for Pithecanthropus.

with large, jutting teeth, no forehead at all and only a tiny brain. Yet another example of *Pithecanthropus* was found in Tanzania in East Africa, in 1945. Soon after, others were discovered there. The important thing about many of these skeletons is that they were found with remains of simple stone tools, fire, and the bones of animals that had been hunted and eaten. Clearly they were not apes.

Scientists gave up using the term *Pithecanthropus* Instead, they called these early beings *Homo erectus* and said they were the ancestors of modern people, or *Homo sapiens*. Most also believed that even *Homo sapiens* had gone through changes. For instance, Neanderthal Man is thought to be an early form of *Homo sapiens* which gave way to modern human beings somewhere around the last Ice Age.

HOW THE EARLY STONE-CUTTERS WORKED

When a prehistoric site is first uncovered all it usually tells is something very obvious such as that people came here and made a fire, worked stone, built a hut or killed certain animals. Dating the remains may be quite easy (see page 74) but working out how people lived, how they did certain jobs and how long it took is very much harder. In recent years archaeologists have been trying to do this by various methods which are all part of 'experimental archaeology'.

Hands and stone

One of the tasks at a prehistoric site is to collect carefully every single piece of stone, from the most elaborate tools to

The Lascaux caves in France were opened to the public in 1952 but it was soon realised that the breathing of the great number of visitors was enough to destroy the paintings. So the site was closed, and a copy of the caves built nearby with reproductions of the paintings as they were made over 12,000 years ago.

the tiniest splinters. This is the first step towards putting all the pieces which made up a tool back together again. At the same time archaeologists study the area where the stone was worked to discover whether the flint came from somewhere else, and whether the work was done in more than one place.

Another type of experimental archaeology is to try to find out how tools were used. This begins with careful examination. On the sharp edges of a tool, there may be traces of the material it was used on. It is often possible to see from these

traces whether the tool was used to scrape fresh skin or dried leather, or whether it was used for hammering, chopping or cutting animal bones, horns, wood or plants. Careful examination will also show whether the stone was fitted to a handle.

After examination comes experiment. Archaeologists have found that it takes only a few minutes to cut a simple, two-faced cutting tool, but up to half a day to make a knife with a laurel-patterned blade. When they have made tools, they can go on to try to use them and discover how the flint was held and which angle makes the best cut. In some sites it is even possible to show the different styles of stoneworkers and work out which objects each one made.

Archaeologists believe they now know how to cut down a tree with a stone axe. The best method is the one the prehistoric people used, which is to strike the trunk at a very slanted angle so that the stone goes in only a short way with each blow. From timber-cutting it was only a short step to trying to build houses like those of Neolithic times. There are several of these reproductions standing in different parts of Europe.

An experiment to show how prehistoric stoneworkers struck blades from a flint core.

Hunting
and painting

Modern archaeologists have carried out other experiments to see whether it is possible to imitate the actions of prehistoric hunters. For example, they will make a bone spearhead and tie it to a wooden shaft using the materials they think were available to early people. They throw it at a hunk of butcher's meat to see how far it goes in and whether any traces of the meat are left on the blade. This helps the archaeologists to work out how weapons were used and what to look for on the flints they uncover.

Another experiment which helps archaeologists in their careful examination of remains is to cut up animal carcasses in different ways to see which marks left on the bones are the same as those found on the sites.

Some experimenters have tried their hand at rock carvings. From this, they can tell us that the oldest pictures in the caves of the Dordogne in France were made simply by striking the rock with a flint point.

Many people have used modern techniques to copy paintings found in caves but some archaeologists have tried to imitate the work of the people who first made them. Their first task was to find the plant which gave the sort of fibres that early people tied together into a simple form of brush. They then set about copying one of the painted cave walls at Peche-Merle in France. Their most striking discovery was that the whole painting could have been completed in not much more than an hour.

Present-day experimenters have succeeded in copying the actions of stoneworkers of the New and Old Stone Ages. From top to bottom:
The researcher is using a hard, wooden hammer to strike blades from a flint core.

Using a piece of wood tipped with bone to press down hard on a prepared core. This is known as pressure-flaking, and makes a much finer and sharper tool.

Using a wooden hammer and bone punch is another way of giving a fine edge to flint blades.

One of the first methods of knapping blades from a core was to use a hammerstone to strike the flint.

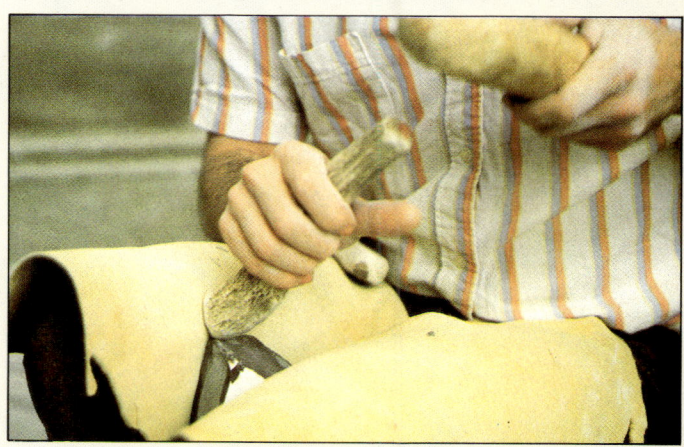

FARMERS AND METALWORKERS, 3,000 YEARS AGO

Several groups of archaeologists in America and Europe have been trying to use their finds to copy the ways in which prehistoric farmers grew crops and cared for animals. In north Germany a curious wooden implement, 6,000 years old, was found. It had a long handle, with a hole on each side, fixed to a blade which was nearly triangular. The archaeologists made a copy and tried to work out how to use it. It was very poor as a spade so they decided it must have been used as a simple kind of plough. When a thong was tied through the two holes they found that one person could pull while another held the handle. Working like this, the implement could dig shallow furrows in the ground.

A farm has been built at Butser Hill as it might have been in the first century BC.

Real ploughs first appeared at the end of the Neolithic Age and in the Bronze Age which followed. There are pictures of them in many rock carvings. Some actual ploughs have been discovered in peat bogs, and these have been copied. In Denmark, experimenters tried harnessing a plough to two oxen as shown in the rock carvings. It worked quite well in light, sandy soil but was much more difficult to use in heavy earth. Even on the light soil, the ploughshare or blade often broke and it seems that prehistoric farmers would have had to fit a new blade six times to plough half a hectare.

The most thorough and long-lasting experiment was the Butser Ancient Farm Research Project in Hampshire, England. It was based on archaeological finds which dated to the first century BC. The experimenters took over twenty-three hectares of land and cleared some fields as well as putting up two circular buildings, workshops, ovens, storage pits, middens and enclosures for animals. Their aim was to discover how everything worked and to follow as closely as possible the way of life of these early farmers. They used copies of prehistoric ploughs and spades, and grew the cereal crops of the first century BC. These were early types of wheat called einkorn and spelt. The experimenters were surprised at the results, because they managed to grow twenty sheaves to 0.6 of a hectare. Even today, with modern seed and the latest equipment, a good crop would be only sixty sheaves from the same area of land. They also found that bread made with these ancient wheats had twice as

Metal being cast as in the time of the first metal-workers.

A present-day experiment near Beaune in France, using copies of Iron-Age furnaces.

much body-building protein as bread made with modern wheat.

The experimenters also kept animals. To plough, they trained some Dexter cattle which were the same size and had the same long legs as skeletons found in ancient sites. Their sheep were Soays which are small, light and rather goat-like, as prehistoric sheep were. The sheep provided meat, milk and a very soft wool that was obtained by pulling it from the animals' backs not by shearing. The experimenters straightened the threads and spun the wool in the Iron Age way. They even made clothes from it. They also herded Exmoor ponies which are the same size as the horses used by Iron Age Celts, and they kept pigs that were partly bred from boars.

Metalworking

Other archaeologists have set out to rediscover how prehistoric people made the bronze and iron goods which are found in sites. Experiments at Beaune in France show that it must have taken early metalworkers a very long time to discover how to produce pure copper from the ore. It was easier to obtain tin because it will run from the ore when it is heated over a charcoal fire. But then came the problem of finding the best proportion of tin to add to copper to make bronze.

After they succeeded in making bronze, the researchers had to work it into the shape they wanted. The simplest method was to beat it into a flat sheet on a series of anvils. They could then beat and bend the sheet into the shapes of vases, cooking pots, goblets and so on. It was much harder to make shapes in moulds. The most delicate shapes were made by a method that prehistoric people used, known as lost wax casting. To start with, the article's shape was modelled in wax fixed over a clay core. The wax was then covered with another layer of clay which had holes bored in it. The whole model was then baked so that the clay hardened but the wax melted and drained through the holes. This left a space between the clay core and the outer shell of clay. The metal was heated until it was liquid, and poured into the space. When it was cool, the clay was broken off, leaving the metal object.

For iron-working, the Beaune experiments used chimney-shaped furnaces. At the bottom, they left holes where air could be blown in with animal-skin bellows. Above the air holes was a closed funnel, a metre or so high. The broad base was packed with charcoal, and the funnel was filled with layers of iron ore mixed with charcoal. When the fire was lit, the ore melted and fell to the bottom. The iron remained as a lump, or 'bloom', in the funnel. It was taken out and toughened by reheating and hammering many times, until it turned into a bar of iron which could be used to make tools.

PUTTING A DATE ON THE PAST

There are two questions to ask when you try to put a date on anything from the past. First, in what order did events happen? Second, when did each of these events happen?

Relative dating

Answers to the first question are called relative dating. The historian or the archaeologist puts events in order, in relation to each other. For prehistoric times, relative dating started with geology. As long ago as 1669, a Danish doctor, Nicholas Steno, was studying rocks in north Italy. He noted that they were divided into several layers, or 'strata', and realised that each layer was made up of mud, or sediment, which had once been at the bottom of the sea. It was obvious that the bottom layer must have been created before others were laid on top of it, so it was the oldest and the top layer was the youngest.

This was the start of the so-called stratigraphic method. Paleontologists, or fossil experts, can add information about the age of strata because they know in which order different creatures appeared before they were fossilised. Archaeologists can take stratigraphic dating even further by looking at the different layers of remains such as bones, ashes or pieces of stone. Again, the oldest remains are in the bottom layer. There is one cave in eastern France where the layers tell us that it was occupied eight times in one century, far back in the Old Stone Age.

Absolute dating

The second question about dating is: when did something happen? Working out the answer is called absolute dating. For events far back in prehistoric times, the most common methods use chemical elements which are radioactive. Carbon 14, for example, is an isotope (an atom of carbon which can be measured separately) which is found in plant and animal life. It is also radioactive. Half the radioactivity in Carbon 14 decays every 5,730 years. This is called its 'half-life'. Scientists can measure the amount of radioactivity in any remain, such as a piece of skin or wood, which was once living.

Stratigraphy is the study of strata, or layers, of rock or remains in prehistoric sites. It tells the order in which the rocks were formed or in which early people made a settlement.

When they know how much is left, they can work out how old the object is by calculating the number of half-lives that have been lost.

Scientists cannot use Carbon 14 to date objects a million years old because nearly all the radioactivity has disappeared. Sometimes they use potassium-argon dating instead. Potassium is one of the basic chemicals, or elements, found in rocks as well as in all living things. It decays to produce calcium and a gas known as argon-40 which has a half-life of 1.3 billion years. The amount of potassium and argon-40 in a rock will show how long the potassium has been decaying. With this information it is possible to date rocks as old as 10 million years. These include the oldest igneous, or heat-formed, rocks on earth and the rocks on the moon. With rocks which go so far back it is impossible to give a completely accurate date, so scientists always give the result with what they think is the margin of error — plus or minus so many thousands of years.

Another help to absolute dating is the study of tree-rings, known as dendro-

Taking a sample of soil to find the direction of the magnetic field at the time when the layer of earth was formed. This is called archaeomagnetism.

chronology. Each year a tree trunk grows another ring, and counting the number of rings tells you the age of the tree. Sometimes hard woods such as oak have been preserved in peat bogs and lakes. If scientists know the rough date from a method such as Carbon 14 dating, it is sometimes possible to get nearer to the actual date by measuring the rings on a tree which may have lived for a hundred or more years 6-7,000 years ago.

Objects affected by great heat can be measured in another way. This method is called thermoluminescence and is the study of the amount of light given off by an object that has been burned. It is used for volcanic rocks and prehistoric remains such as hearth stones.

Even the study of magnetism can help dating. Some metals show the direction of the magnetic field at the time when they were formed. Today the magnetic field makes compasses point to magnetic north, a few degrees away from the North Pole. Three quarters of a million years ago the needle would have pointed to the south, and between then and now it has had many different positions. There is a science called archaeomagnetism which uses special equipment to find the magnetic field of old rocks. They can then be dated by what is known of the magnetic field at different times in the earth's long history.

Potassium-argon dating. The scientist is using a spectrometer to measure how much argon-40 gas has been produced by the decay of potassium in a rock.

CHRONOLOGY

Thousands of Years Ago B.C.	Europe	Middle East-Eastern Mediterranean	Americas	Africa-Asia Oceania
30,000	Earliest cave art in France and Spain The last Neanderthals Rise of Cro-Magnons First bone and ivory carved figures		Asian hunters cross Bering Strait	Australia populated
25,000	First goddess statuettes			
20,000	Invention of needle Sungir graves	Ice Age at its peak		First cave art in Australia
15,000	Lascaux cave paintings Invention of harpoon			
13,000	Pincevent			
12,000			Spread of cave art in Brazil	
10,000		**End of Ice Age**		
9000	Invention of bow and arrow	First boats on Mediterranean First villages in Syria/Palestine (Jericho, Mallaha, Mureybet, etc.)	Folsom stonework	
8000		First baked clay figurines Agriculture begins		Pottery first made in Japan
7000		Copper beads (Turkey) Loom invented	First domesticated plants (gourds)	
6000	Agriculture spreads through Mediterranean and begins to replace hunting	Catal Hüyük becomes largest city		First cave art in Tassili caves in Algeria
5000	Agriculture spreads to Danube region First megaliths built in Brittany		Corn cultivated in Mexico	
4000	First lake villages	**Very temperate climate** Copper working First cities Wheel develops Beginnings of writing	First pottery develops on Pacific coast Alpaca domesticated in Andes	
3000	First gold and copper beads Stonehenge begun in England	Bronze Age begins Plough developed First pyramids built in Egypt	First farmers settle in Central America	Indus civilisation rises
2500				Sahara begins to dry
2000	Use of bronze begins	Cretan civilisation Iron Age begins	Farming becomes main way of life in Central America	
1000	Use of iron begins			

INDEX

A mammoth skeleton in the palaeontology exhibit at the Natural History Museum in Paris, France.

Aisne valley

Ko

Tamaulipas

Tehuacan valley

Ahaggar
Adrar Bous
Aïr

Huaca Prieta
Lima sites

Telamarchay